Cecilia. The Story of a Girl and some Circumstances.

Stanley Victor Makower

CECILIA

CECILIA

The Story of a Girl and Some Circumstances

BY

STANLEY V. MAKOWER

JOHN LANE: THE BODLEY HEAD

LONDON AND NEW YORK

1897

𝔘𝔫𝔦𝔳𝔢𝔯𝔰𝔦𝔱𝔶 𝔓𝔯𝔢𝔰𝔰

John Wilson and Son, Cambridge, U.S.A.

TO ONE BOTH SEVERE AND GENTLE,

A WIT WITHOUT MALICE,

A CRITIC AND A FRIEND,

THIS BOOK IS DEDICATED.

CECILIA

Part I

I

CECILIA DAVENPORT RAYNER had been the
centre of attraction in Emilienbad for six consecutive weeks, during which she had danced,
flirted, and acted in what were euphemistically
called " private " theatricals to an audience consisting of the most distinguished excrescences
from all the Courts of Europe.

Monsieur de Pommarion, who was as well
known in the little watering-place as the old
tree in front of the Hôtel du Rhin, had once
gone so far as to compare Miss Rayner (inac-
curately enough) to a mistress of the first
Napoleon with whom, when he was quite a
youth, just seventy years ago, he had enjoyed
an intimacy that had since become historical.

Cecilia

The comparison was not wasted: for at the next full ball at the Casino the flattered young lady appeared in a costume, the bodice of which, executed with great care from fashion plates sent from Paris, was designed to suggest Gérard's famous portrait of Mademoiselle George. On that evening it was noticed that Madame de Rampazzi, another familiar figure, whose age was about eighty, and who had hitherto preserved a unique distinction by appearing in a white satin dress of the period of the first Empire, studded with historic jewels, retired rather earlier than usual, and the motion of her fan, as she waved it to and fro in front of her enamelled bosom, betrayed malice in its rhythm, while with an infinitesimal portion of her once beautiful eyes she sat scrutinising the movements of Miss Rayner.

Graf Dornstein, attaché to the Austrian Ambassador in Paris, was perhaps the favourite among Miss Rayner's evening cavaliers. His age was forty; he was of rather less than the average height, and his movements, which were quick and impulsive, carried with them a certain swagger.

His well-proportioned figure, always set off by clothes which fitted perfectly, though they were of a decidedly foreign cut, suggested a tailor-made elegance rather than any natural strength or beauty of physique. His thin head sat arrogantly upon shoulders slightly narrow; the eyes were close together and wore a somewhat fierce, restless expression, which changed to one of animation when he was speaking, but which, when he was silent and alone, had secured for him among the crowd of gossips outside the circle of his own acquaintance the reputation of a fiery temper. The suddenness with which he would from time to time pass his hand over his perfectly trimmed imperial beard strengthened this impression. Certainly his hand alone would have gained him distinction among the ladies, for it was thin and pale, with the most irreproachable nails, which were polished and whitened until they positively shone with the lustre of rare gems. Moreover he danced exquisitely, and his feet were very small.

Dornstein gambled regularly from midnight until three, four, or five in the morning, so that it was quite impossible for him to present an attractive appearance at the Springs at so early an hour as seven o'clock; but the delicious, feathery white costume of Miss Rayner could always be seen from a long way off fluttering and trembling through the alley of lime-trees which led to the Elizabethenquelle. It was part of the exquisite scene which unfolded itself morning after morning of the hot summer of '86.

Miss Rayner's morning cavalier was the second son of the Earl of Badminton, the honourable Hubert, who had just come down from Cambridge in consequence of a repeated failure to pass his Little Go. His chief qualifications for so distinguished an office as the companionship of Miss Rayner were a superb waistcoat and buff gaiters (with pale-blue stars at discreet intervals), which were the admiration of all Emilienbad.

The honourable Hubert never said very much; but he looked fresh and pleasant in the morning, and he never forgot to present Miss Rayner with a bunch of damask roses, bought at the little flower stall at the end of the alley of limes. This was the only bunch of that colour in Emilienbad, with the exception of that especially reserved for the Princess Nekrasoff.

"You are too good," Cecilia always said; and the young man's rosy face blushed a little deeper, that was all. Conversation would, in fact, have been superfluous. Far more enjoyment was to be obtained by silently wandering in and out of the pretty crowd of people, recognising the fragments of popular melodies which floated in and out of the branches of the trees, — now faint, now stronger, but always distant, — and watching the kaleido-scopic, ever-varying combinations of acquaint-ances which each new day revealed as the season advanced.

In grateful contrast to the middle of the day, when the heat was so intense that people could do nothing but sit in darkened rooms waiting for the sun to go down, the air of the early morning was deliciously cool. The grass was sprinkled with dew which quivered here and there with the rays of the sun, and from the intermingling of the natural beauty of the scene with the artificial elegance of the crowd, and the facile sparkle of conventional phrases in the music tossed lightly on the ear, arose a vague, mysterious charm which seemed to clothe with grace, every gesture, every bow of recognition, every smile. Men and women moved and talked with an infinite propriety, always forming fresh groups, which grew and grew, and then melted away.

At eight o'clock every morning, a photograph was taken of the Elizabethenquelle, round which all the fashionable world gathered, whether they drank the waters or not. Miss Rayner always chanced to appear in the centre, standing next to a stone image of a boy blowing a stone trumpet; one of his legs was raised as if in the pathetic endeavour to waft his stone body into the sky overhead. Curiously enough, in close proximity to Miss Rayner, was usually to be seen the King of the Netherlands, and one or two other crowned heads, seduced into notoriety by the cunning of the photographer, who exhibited a specimen of his work every day in the handsome window of his shop, Hochstrasse, No. 10.

The season was very gay indeed. The weather during the whole time was perfect, and not a day went by without a ball, theatricals, a tennis party, or some public event in which Cecilia reigned supreme. At a concert given in the Casino, she sang divinely.

Cecilia

"How nervous I shall be," she had said modestly, a few days before, to which Dornstein had gallantly answered, in that broken English which everybody agreed was so charming, that the Queen was never nervous of her subjects, but that, to give her courage, they would form a royal court in front of the platform and cheer Her Majesty.

Accordingly, a distinguished little party of Miss Rayner's friends, organised by the fascinating Austrian, had taken the whole front row of the stalls.

She appeared in a lovely, soft, silk dress, couleur de rose, unadorned by any jewels. Raising her cheek and slightly moving her lips so as to invite a momentary glance at a beautiful row of teeth, she bowed to the audience, while she gazed vaguely down the long room in search of familiar faces. Then she stood perfectly still, and her eyes brightened as she looked, first at Dornstein, and then at the Prince Pezarin, who was of the Count's party.

Out of compliment to the Prince, she sang "Te souviens-tu?" remembering that he had once told her that it was his favourite song. She retired amidst a storm of applause, to make way for Señor da Gamba, who played one of his own fantasias on the 'cello.

Something like a glimmer of approbation shone in the glassy eyes of Monsieur de Pommarion when he observed Cecilia reappear later in the programme, in her new ball costume. The distinguished-looking friend of Napoleon sat in a corner of the room, resting his handsome head, with its cluster of snow-white curls, on his hands, which were folded over the knob of a thin, old silver cane.

This time she sang "Ich liebe Dich," in compliment to Count Dornstein, who was enraptured, and clapped his hands in between the verses, crying, "Brava." She had to appear three times to satisfy the audience, and finally retired, half hidden by an immense basket of flowers, of which the handle, covered with roses, nearly reached her shoulder. It was presented by the Count, amidst a furore of clapping.

The orchestra had begun to tune their instruments for the overture of "Ruy Blas," with which the concert was to conclude, when Cecilia, having rapidly thrown a lace shawl round her shoulders, stole round to the audience. The whole of the front row at once showed their admiration and curiosity by offering the singer imaginary empty seats and leaning in her direction. Finally, room was found for her between Dornstein and the Prince, who sat at the end of the row. The mother of the young lady, Mrs. Rayner, who occupied a seat towards the middle, cried out : —

" Cecilia, my dear Cecilia!" in a voice that could be taken to denote an irrelevant burst of affection, or that she had something important to say. But Cecilia appeared not to hear, being suddenly much pre-occupied with the arrangement of her shawl, which had caught in a pin, and which Dornstein was eagerly trying to detach for her. Her mother, baffled, subsided into a whispered conversation with an old lady who was on her left.

Although nearly sixty years of age, and very stout, this lady wore a low-necked black-silk dress; and upon her fat, lugubrious face was impressed a look of permanent surprise, due chiefly to her eyes, which were clear and vacant like those of a baby. Her head was covered with a sober wig of dark hair, parted in the middle, and half hiding her large ears, at the side of which two tufts of thin, grizzled hair recklessly protruded themselves, as if to give the final lie to any one who for a moment might be deceived into accepting those folds of thick, brown hair as Miss Savory's own. The wig was surmounted by a small heap of cream-coloured lace and ruby velvet. Upon her ample bosom, which heaved complacently up and down as she breathed, lay a large, oval locket in gold.

Miss Savory was the daughter of a doctor in Exeter, where she spent the first half of her life, and where Mrs. Rayner, then Miss Panton, was her chief companion at school. At the age of twenty-five, she lost both her father and mother, and after starting a seminary for young ladies, which she conducted for some years with considerable trouble and little satisfaction, she determined to follow Miss Panton's example, and go to London, with the object of seeking a post as resident governess or companion in a family.

But by this time, a lugubriousness had spread over her character which stood in the way of her success. She was too mournful to be a desirable governess or an agreeable companion, and she met with no satisfactory offers. She accordingly contented herself with living on the money which had been left her, and to which she added a small sum, gathered from private lessons which she gave in Drawing, Music, and The Higher Orthography.

Quite recently she had received an unexpected legacy of five thousand pounds, and, thanks to this accession of wealth, she felt justified in taking a cure at Emilienbad, to which place she had been advised to go, by the doctors.

Only twice had any passion disturbed the sordid uneventfulness of her life: once when she was seventeen, before her lugubriousness had had time to assert itself, and once, only ten years ago, when she surprised herself in the act of kissing the photograph of an old friend to whom she always alluded as the Colonel. But in neither case did the affair end in matrimony. For the youthful lover died suddenly, and the remembrance of that early romance lasted nearly thirty years, at the end of which the image of the youth became so faint and used, that she sought to revive it in a new form; but the Colonel, suspecting the condition of Miss Savory's affections, openly declared his abhorrence of married life, and the elderly lady only sighed and pressed his hand a little more warmly when he took leave of her on that occasion.

Miss Savory possessed a language of her own, possibly the survival of a habit contracted long ago when she was at the head of the seminary; it resembled the clucking of a hen, and she substituted it at random for the more usual methods of conversation, though it was often difficult to guess precisely what it signified.

At this moment, it seemed sometimes to denote amusement, sometimes acquiescence in a remark of Mrs. Rayner, while sometimes it seemed to be used merely as a bridge wherewith to span gaps in their conversation. They had not been talking for long, however, when they were interrupted by the rapping of the conductor's stick on the desk, followed by the vague hum of diminishing voices as people settled into their seats, and the single figures standing up here and there sank into the compact mass of the audience.

After a brilliant performance of the over-ture, the people began to leave the concert-room : first in knots of two or three, then one by one, — as water leaks through a crack, now in a stream, now drop by drop.

" I am going to stay here a little while, till I am quite cool," said Cecilia to her mother, who was one of the last to leave the room. " You will take care of me, won't you, Count Dornstein ? " she added, turning as with a sudden inspiration to the delighted favourite, with whom, after an appropriate amount of hesitation, she had agreed to sing a duet as soon as everybody had left the room.

" Be sure you don't catch cold, my child," said Mrs. Rayner, with a fresh burst of irre-levant affection. " You will look after her, Count, won't you ? " And she laid her hand,

as if inadvertently, on the arm of Dornstein,
who reassured her in his best broken English.

A faint perfume which hung in the air, and
here and there a broken line of chairs where
people had forced a way out, were all that now
were left to suggest that the room had, but a
few moments ago, been full of people.

Cecilia sat on a chair in the deserted front
row, leaning back languidly, as if fatigued with
her exertions; and the Count sauntered about
humming under his breath the melody of " Ich
liebe Dich," and breaking now and then into a
rather more vehement rendering of a phrase
with a wave of his hand, then relapsing into a
drowsy, subterranean sound.

A liveried servant came in and pushed the
chairs into their position. They made a harsh,
resounding noise as they scraped along the parquet floor. When he had restored them all to
their places, he took a long pole from a dark
corner, and walked all round, turning out the

brilliant jets of gas which ornamented the walls. The Count glared at him as he turned out the last jet at the further end of the room.

Only two flames, close to the piano on the platform, were now left alight, and towards these the Count groped his way, while the noise of a door banging close to him told him that the servant had left the room. The orchestra had gone to play in the open pavilion in the gardens until a little before twelve o'clock, when the ball was to begin. A single figure was left, that of a boy who was putting a double bass into a cover.

By the time the Count reached the platform, Cecilia, at the piano, was caressing a faint sound out of the keys. When he heard the piano, the boy stopped with the cover in his hand, but, on meeting the fierce gaze of Dornstein, hurried the instrument into its case and vanished down the mysterious hole in the platform, through which the performers had a little while ago appeared.

Cecilia

As soon as he was gone, Miss Rayner dispelled the gloomy silence of the great, dark, empty room by a brilliant caprice on " Faust," while Dornstein caught up such melodies as were familiar to him, and sang them in French, growing quite excited with the music, and performing many of the conventional gestures which accompany singing on the stage, starting back with both hands on his chest, taking short strides and clasping his hands together passionately, and so on. When they came to the love duet, Cecilia herself began to sing, and Dornstein, whose voice was powerful rather than beautiful, fairly roared. Cecilia also had to scream a little to make herself heard, and at the finale, which both singers performed with great spirit, Cecilia clapped her hands and burst into a loud peal of laughter, and, as it died down into a ripple, it mingled with the faint blare of the orchestra which floated over the illuminated gardens, through the open window.

Cecilia

The Count was a little perplexed at the rippling laughter of Cecilia.

"But it's such fun," she cried, breaking out again, and swaying from side to side until a rose tumbled from her hair, which the Count's face brushed as he stooped to pick up the flower.

"How well it went, and what a beautiful voice—" She stopped as if afraid to pay him so direct a compliment.

Meanwhile, an immense throng had assembled round the pavilion in the gardens of the Casino, and along the main paths which led to it. All the seats were taken, and people, in groups of two and three, were walking in full evening dress in and out of fairy lights that wound along the border of the grass plots in chains of blue, yellow, and red. Conspicuous among the crowd was the erect figure of Prince Pezarin as he stood beside the bent form of Monsieur de Pommarion, with whom he was exchanging a few words.

Cecilia

The Prince, who was fifty years of age, was tall and dark, with small, dark, piercing eyes, and a moustache that was waxed into two stiff points that looked like needles as they sprang from each end of his rather colourless lips. He was dressed immaculately in ultra-English style. He had had an English nurse as a child, and as a young man had been a passionate admirer of Lord Byron. He could speak Russian, French, and English with equal fluency, but preferred a combination of French and English, both of which he pronounced as if they were his native tongue; but he affected an essentially English deliberateness of manner, both in speaking and in moving. He never hurried. Four fingers of his right hand were usually in the cross pocket of his coat, into which his thumb was never allowed to enter. That always lay outside the pocket, the corner of which was slightly baggy from the tension on the stuff which the habit involved; but the creases were rarely visible, for his thumb nearly always covered them. In his left hand, the little finger of which was adorned with a gold ring set with a single amber-coloured stone, he usually carried a cigar, more rarely an elegant walking-stick of clear horn with a small finely chased silver top, which he always held in the middle, never allowing it to touch the ground.

Monsieur de Pommarion, his throat wrapped round and round with a wrapper, soon left the Prince, and walked with bent back and slow tottering steps down a solitary path; and Pezarin, bored with the noise and the constant stream of people, made his way towards the Casino, which, for the time, was deserted. He paused to strike a match on the bark of a tree, swiftly lit a large cigar which he had drawn from his pocket, and then wandered out of sight of the crowd, until he was far enough away for the noise of the orchestra not to distress him.

He happened to pass in front of the open window of the concert-room at the moment when Dornstein was stooping to pick up the rose that had fallen from Cecilia's hair. The picture amused him, and he smiled as he passed on, mentally noting the circumstance. It neither surprised nor vexed him; it only aroused in him the memory of his own early life.

His experience of watering-places dated over thirty years, ever since, as a boy of twenty, he started his career at Aix-les-bains by falling in love with a provincial actress. So passionately attached to her was he, that he had actually promised to marry her, a catastrophe which was only averted by the promptitude and ingenuity of his father, who rushed round to the young lady's lodgings early on the very morning on which the ceremony was to have taken place, and swore that his son was a beggar, and would never have a single kopek if he persisted in carrying out his crazy intention. At the same time, he offered the bewildered Therese Melany five thousand marks down, if she would leave Aix by the very next train, which started in one hour. The Melany held out for another thousand marks, and concluded the bargain; for, though at a later period she made a notorious success in Berlin in light rôles, at the time of this episode she could not afford to throw away the money. She left at ten o'clock; and when the young Prince climbed the five flights of stairs an hour later, he found the dirty little room all disordered, and the owner gone. On the table was a faded bouquet, his own gift of a week ago, the ribbons all twisted and bedraggled, and beside it lay a stage dagger, which, in her hurry to catch the train, the actress had forgotten to put into her trunk. Had there been a river in Aix, the young Prince would have thrown himself into it, as he threatened his father, whom he suspected of being an accomplice in the flight. As it was, he contented himself with stabbing himself with the stage dagger, which, in spite of repeated essays, would never penetrate further than his waistcoat, though he succeeded in alarming his father with it on the occasion of the first attempt.

Reminiscences of this kind arose to the Prince's memory, adding a serene joy and sense of present well-being to the flavour of his cigar, from which he was blowing clouds of heavy, blue smoke that curled lazily into phantastic shapes in the cool evening air. He was just wandering back to the pavilion, unconsciously attracted by the lights and the crowd of people, when two figures passed him, and, looking back, greeted him with a little cry of surprise.

Cecilia was the first to speak.

" Ah! Prince Pezarin, do you know where mamma is? I 'm quite cool now, and I want to go to her."

Pezarin answered that he had seen her sitting near the pavilion; and Dornstein, anxious to be off, for he had arrangements still to make in connection with the ball, bowed, and, returning to the Casino, left Cecilia with the Prince.

They wandered over the grass, away from the main stream of the people, until they came to a seat under a tree whose branches hung over a solitary path lined with lights that shone like jewels. Cecilia seemed to have forgotten that she wanted to see her mother, and they both sat down.

"You sang divinely to-night," said the Prince. Cecilia did not answer. She only loosened her cloak and allowed her fingers to stray over her bodice, till they rested in the pose assumed by those of the actress in Gérard's picture. She then sighed and looked up through the branches of the tree at the clusters of stars overhead.

"Why is 'Te souviens-tu?' your favourite song?" she said at last, without moving.

"Affaire de cœur——" said the Prince, dropping the stump of his cigar upon the edge of the grass, and following it with his eyes to where it lay between his feet, a tiny circle of glowing fire.

"I once killed a man on account of that song," he went on.

"Killed a man?" echoed Cecilia, faintly.

"He pushed past me at a concert in Pétersbourg at which Bianca sang," he continued.

"Who was Bianca?"

"Bianca Malvini,—the famous Malvini. Dieu de dieux, what a voice she had! The whole world went mad over her. She sang that song with her eyes closed the whole time," the Prince went on meditatively.

"And why did you kill the poor man?" said Cecilia, compassionately.

"Why? Why? He lost his head, pushed past me, and knocked my arm. He wanted to go behind the stage to congratulate her; but I seized him by the collar and held him. 'Mademoiselle n'est pas libre, monsieur,' I said. He looked as if he would eat me. We met the next morning. What choice had I? And I killed him."

"Poor fellow — how cruel of you," said Cecilia, still looking up through the branches of the trees. "And was she very, very beautiful?"

"An angel," murmured the Prince.

"How wonderful, how romantic!" said Cecilia, earnestly. "Ah, Russia must be a lovely country. How I would love to live there — Pétersbourg — Pétersbourg," she went on with a pretty imitation of the Prince's pronunciation. "Ah, Pétersbourg must be rippish." She half drowned the word, which was one of her own invention, in a stream of silvery laughter, so that it sounded mysterious and strangely fascinating. Then she stopped, looked down, and began to trace patterns in the sand with her dainty little foot, which was clad in the sweetest of white satin shoes.

The Prince preserved an icy silence for some minutes; and Cecilia suddenly remembered that her mother must be wondering what had become of her.

" What time is it ? " she asked as she rose.

" Nearly twelve," said the Prince.

" I had no idea it was so late. Will you take me at once to mamma ? "

Pezarin offered her his arm in reply, and they walked away together. Soon they caught sight of Mrs. Rayner and Miss Savory, who were sitting near the pavilion earnestly engaged in conversation, of which the following fragment reached them as they made their way towards the two ladies.

" Impossible," said Miss Savory, incredulously.

" It's a fact," answered Mrs. Rayner, emphatically, following with her eyes the figure of a handsome woman of middle age who had just passed. " Our chambermaid heard it from her maid."

" What a horrible idea ! " said Miss Savory, impressively.

Cecilia

" Is n't it terrible ?   I think it perfectly terrible !" Mrs. Rayner went on mechanically,
whilst she still pursued with her eyes the diminishing figure of the lady whom they were
discussing.

Miss Savory clucked. She made a queer
noise in her throat, and then a sound something like that of innumerable m's jostling each
other, without any vowels between them, then
another queer noise, then more m's.

" Ah, Cecilia," said Mrs. Rayner, suddenly,
" my dear Cecilia, how wicked of you to keep
away so long. What have you been doing?
Prince, what has she been doing?" she added,
as the two appeared before her, cutting off
her view, and exciting a paroxysm of maternal
solicitude.

Cecilia did not answer, and the Prince only
smiled a little disdainfully.

" Let us come to the Casino," he said, " or
we shall be late for the ball."

So the two ladies rose; and they all walked

to the hot, brilliantly lighted room in which people were already beginning to gather in crowds.

The dance commenced at midnight; and, as a preliminary ceremony, twelve chimes were struck on a silver bell by the leader of the orchestra, to the wonder and delight of the people. It was the greatest success of the season, and the handsome room was crammed with the élite of Emilienbad. An English prince was seen for five minutes taking a glass of lemonade in the refreshment-room, and every one whispered to every one else that he had just seen the royal personage, commenting with surprise upon his stoutness, and lending weight to the observation by a statement of the distance (carelessly described as a stone's throw) from which the speaker had been enabled to gather his interesting impression. But the triumph of the evening was a short and brilliant cotillon led by Graf Dornstein, whose taste and invention were on everybody's lips.

Cecilia

There were six figures, the prettiest being that in which all the gentlemen wore pale-blue satin dress-coats with a scarlet ribbon flowing from the left shoulder. The ladies were presented with pieces of ribbon which corresponded in length to those sewn upon the gentlemen's coats. Those whose ribbons were of exactly the same length danced together, and the fun and confusion while the gentlemen were being measured were indescribable.

Miss Rayner looked positively ravishing as she smiled at the Count, and shook her wrist, which was covered with bracelets, trophies of ribbon, and trinkets of every description. Everybody was madly in love with her; and the next evening Mr. Mark Isidore left with his daughters for Ostende, convinced at last that his wife was right when she argued that neither Rachel nor Rebecca would stand a chance while the fascinating Miss Davenport Rayner remained in Emilienbad.

Cecilia

Cecilia and her mother walked home together through the Casino gardens, across the principal street of the little town, which was so still that the sound of their footsteps on the pavement seemed almost an outrage. Not until they were in their small bedroom on the third floor, did Mrs. Rayner break the silence between them.

"We must go away from here; it's too expensive," she said, positively and sharply.

Cecilia answered:

"Very well, mamma;" but she was gazing abstractedly at the looking-glass, with her hand resting on the pin which she was just going to pull out from the back of her head.

"Twenty pounds a week's preposterous," Mrs. Rayner continued. "Besides we're wasting time. The people are no good. Certainly Graf Dornstein," she added, rather more graciously, for she wanted to provoke from her daughter a declaration of how matters stood. But Cecilia was obstinately silent.

32

Cecilia

"Graf Dornstein? Yes?" she said at last, looking up and pulling the pin from her hair.

"Dances very well," added her mother, determined not to be caught out by the assumed innocence of her daughter.

"Admirably," answered the girl, calmly. "I never enjoyed a dance so much as to-night. Where do you want to go after leaving here?"

"I don't know," said the mother, peevishly. "We can't go on living at this rate much longer. The sitting-room downstairs costs us twenty-seven francs a day, Cecilia. It's preposterous — preposterous."

The bedroom only cost eight francs; but the sitting-room was one of the best in the hotel, being next to that occupied by the Duke of Mecklinburg Strelitz, as Mrs. Rayner would never tire of telling her friends.

Cecilia did not answer; and Mrs. Rayner, stung at last into the aggressive, turned sharply to her daughter, and said in a new voice:

"I don't at all like the way you behave

with Graf Dornstein, Cecilia. Everybody will talk of it."

But Cecilia, who was already in bed, only answered with a yawn, and, "So sleepy, good-night;" and Mrs. Rayner beat a retreat under the sheets to hide the ignominy of her discomfiture.

II

ANOTHER week had been spent in the gay little watering-place, for somehow Mrs. Rayner imagined that, by straining a nerve now, important results might ultimately be obtained which would amount to a life-long economy. So she lingered on, smiling at her daughter in public, and talking bitterly to her when they were alone.

Once, after her usual reproach that Cecilia was not circumspect enough, the girl, who felt instinctively that her mother's protest was merely a veil to disguise something much more characteristic of her than an abhorrence of frivolity, turned sharply round, and in a voice in which was a note of pain, cried :

" What do you want ?   What do you want ? "
The directness of the question disarmed Mrs.

35

Cecilia

Rayner so completely that she took refuge in a burst of tears, talked tragically about a mother's feelings, and at last retreated to her room, to lament and wonder at her daughter's display of temper.

Cecilia was in fact not yet disposed to realise to the full the practical side of the question. She would have liked to find herself, as if by accident, the victim of circumstances which her instinct had only half consciously built up around her. Mrs. Rayner vainly strove to tear from her daughter this last rag of illusion. So long as Cecilia could keep her mother at a distance when she was actually engaged in any little intrigue, she was indifferent; but the active interference of Mrs. Rayner, and her inappropriate innuendoes in the presence of Count Dornstein, wounded the girl, compelling her mind to the precision of something which the better side of her nature prompted her to leave undefined. Moreover, on several occasions the mother's indiscretions very nearly wrecked the whole situation. As it was, everybody laughed about Mrs. Rayner's constant allusions to Lady Bland.

· A little group of people, including the Rayners, were sitting one afternoon in the Casino gardens, and gossiping pleasantly in the shade of the trees, when old Miss Savory, who was secretly known as " the crab," limped up with an expression of pain on her fat, lugubrious face. Room was at once made for her in the circle, and a general inquiry as to her health followed. This was met with the usual explanation, beginning with " My poor leg," when Mrs. Rayner, cutting it short, at once recommended an embrocation of which Lady Bland had told her, and then adroitly pinned on to her recommendation an account of how that dear lady had fallen from a horse and lain on one side for three weeks, until she used the invaluable ointment. From this, an easy transition was effected to the state of Lady Bland's health, her rashness in riding at a breakneck pace in the park without the attendance of a groom, when from so large an establishment as Huntingdon House one could be so easily spared, the distress of Lord Bland when he heard of the accident, the incompetence of the doctors, and finally the letter which Mrs. Rayner had ten days ago received from Lady Bland, to her great relief, for she was really beginning to be anxious.

At this point she stopped in her account, not seeing in her mind any more vistas of conversation with Lady Bland at the end of them. So she rose and emphatically pleaded an engagement, whilst she looked significantly at Cecilia, with whom she retired, amidst many protests.

As soon as they were out of hearing, some one observed very positively, " Why does n't Mrs. Rayner bring Lady Bland with her? I believe she is a myth." And a little shiver of laughter passed over the group, the sound of which reached Cecilia, whose lips quivered a little contemptuously as she walked by the side of her mother.

Remarks of this kind did not do any good. It began even to be whispered that the name was not Rayner at all, but Rehner. The worst discovery, however, was made by Lady Killigrew to an inquisitive circle of friends who were taking tea with her on the following afternoon at the Conditorei.

Lady Killigrew, who was about forty, was extremely handsome. She had a sound knowledge of the world, for whose opinion she professed a frank indifference, while she was far too worldly to defy it openly. Her first husband had drunk himself to death, — so at least society whispered. Lord Killigrew was usually "away shootin';" and her affection for the second son of a duke, with whom she was always seen at race meetings, was charitably accounted for by the discreet legend that he had once saved her life. The facts were unimportant, except to the few who made them up, and who had no object in disclosing them. She lived more in Paris than in London, where she was seen only for a month in the season. All that appeared was, that she was beautiful, knew a great many people (many of them distinguished), and managed her reputation with infinite tact.

Amidst sallies of inextinguishable laughter, she informed the company assembled at the confectioner's shop who Lady Bland was. She was the daughter of a London dressmaker in the West End, called Madame Lejeune. Every one knew Madame Lejeune; she had the most exquisite gowns. Lady Killigrew indicated a marvel of tumbled Brussels point which she was wearing at that moment, as an example of her style. She went on to inform the company that Lejeune's real name was Lazarus, thereby raising a burst of fresh laughter, which was echoed from time to time as the story passed round the crowded little shop, exciting infinite amusement at each table at which people sat eating masterpieces of German confectionery of every shape and colour, and drinking tea or chocolate out of Limoges china.

Fresh material for laughter was afforded in the story of Lazarus, who had bought a constituency in the East End of London, and was now a member of Parliament. Several petitions had been lodged against him, in which he had been charged with corrupt practices; but they had been dropped, one by one, for want of money to prosecute them. Chokes and groans were still to be heard amongst the company, when somebody asked who Lord Bland was.

On the announcement that Lord Bland was a penniless, Irish, non-representative peer, the tea-tables clattered; for every one had heard Mrs. Rayner's constant allusions to the necessity of Lord Bland's presence in the House of Lords.

Lady Killigrew was about to continue with an account of how the marriage between Lord

Bland and Miss Queenie Lazarus had been accomplished, and was just describing, with infinite humour, their first meeting, when Cecilia and her mother entered the shop, and Lady Killigrew, breaking off her description as they advanced towards the table, invited them to come and sit next her and drink a cup of chocolate.

The mother and daughter joined the party, whose attention was at once riveted on them.

"We are leaving in two days," said Mrs. Rayner, as she settled into a seat beside Lady Killigrew, showing her teeth a little, which was her substitute for a smile. The company professed astonishment, and feigned distress.

"Cecilia and I are miserable at the thought of it," continued Mrs. Rayner. "We love the place — just love the place," she cried, lifting her hands a little. "But Cecilia must have change of air — not so relaxing. Lady Bland writes from Glyon to say that it's lovely there. So we think we shall go on at once to keep her company."

When the chorus of regrets on all sides had subsided, Lady Killigrew inquired anxiously after Lady Bland's health; and the delighted Mrs. Rayner gave her the substance of a letter which she had that morning received, adding embellishments of her own, and digressions which were immensely diverting. Soon afterwards, every one rose to go. While Lady Killigrew was paying the bill, Mrs. Rayner became absorbed in conversation with a lady of the party, and it was not until they were at the door of the shop that a well-timed flight of memory enabled her to realise what had taken place, when she broke into vehement expostulation and self-condemnation, begging Lady Killigrew to tell her what her own and Cecilia's chocolate had cost; but Lady Killigrew only smiled, and said she hoped Mrs. Rayner would allow herself and her daughter to be included among her party; and Mrs. Rayner, after pressing the point as far as was compatible with amiable manners, finally submitted with touching resignation.

The news of Cecilia's near departure soon spread, as Mrs. Rayner intended it should. Various reasons had led to her determination, not the least cogent being that if two days could not suffice to bring matters to a head, it was useless wasting any more time and money in Emilienbad.

The next morning, Dornstein appeared for the first time at the Springs, and for the last time that year Cecilia's white dress fluttered along the alley of limes. The beautiful girl was besieged with compliments, and had her choice of at least six different cavaliers for her morning walk. Her triumph culminated in an introduction to the King of Moravia, whose passion for pretty women was notorious. She walked twice up and down with His Majesty, in the full view of all Emilienbad, and then the King, pleading an imperial hunger, left her with

Cecilia

Prince Pezarin, while, with a bow (his left hand, which was fat and covered with rings, planted rakishly at his back), he hurried off to breakfast. It was now the time when the photograph was taken; and Cecilia, surrounded by a little group of admirers, took up her usual position next the stone statue of the boy blowing the trumpet. The honourable Hubert made his way to her with a bunch of damask roses, just in time to be included in the picture. He blushed more deeply than ever, and stuck in the middle of a sentence which he had prepared with infinite trouble, to the effect that when Miss Rayner was gone, there would be nobody in Emilienbad worthy of wearing the red roses, which Cecilia accepted with her usual smile and, —

"You are too good."

To hide his confusion, he was just taking refuge in a glass of bubbling spring water which he held in his hand, when the photographer, giving a cry like that of a general marshalling his forces, opened the shutter of his camera, and then closed it again with a click. The crowd then began to melt away from the Elizabethenquelle in different directions. The Count accompanied Cecilia to the Hôtel du Rhin; for she was so loaded with flowers that she could not carry them all by herself.

"You don't look well, Dornstein," she said, as they left the gardens together. The fact was that the early morning did not suit the Count. He looked pale and haggard, and his pointed beard, which was a marvel of symmetry later in the day, was wild and disordered. He had lost heavily, too, at cards the night before, which gave him a melancholy and dejected air.

"How can I look vell, Miss Raynair, ven your départure is so near?" he asked. Cecilia was silent a moment. Then:

"You must come and see us in London. Mamma has given you our address, and we shall look forward to a visit from you."

Cecilia

" Ah, London, London," he said absently, as if he were thinking over something in his mind which gave him considerable difficulty. He had almost passed by the hotel door, when Cecilia, stopping, offered him her hand.

" For the last time," he said, bowing over it gallantly, and kissing the tips of her fingers. He looked up and sighed disconsolately.

" And the Casino? Will you be there to-night? " he said.

" I 'm afraid we shall have to pack to-night," replied Cecilia. " We leave early to-morrow morning." She held out her arms for the flowers, which he piled up as best he could. A rose fell on the pavement, over which the shadow of the tree opposite the hotel swayed to and fro.

" You permit me to keep it? " he said, as he stooped to pick it up. The scene in the concert-room of the Casino rose in Cecilia's mind, as she broke into a ripple of laughter, and said, " Certainly ! "

Two little boys in tight cloth suits, adorned with innumerable brass buttons, raised their caps, which bore "Hôtel du Rhin" upon them in handsome gold letters, and held open the great glass doors for Cecilia, as she went up the steps and passed into the hall.

Dornstein waved his grey felt hat until Miss Rayner passed out of sight; then he turned away and walked slowly down the little street that was already glaring white under the morning sun. He chewed the stem of the rose between his teeth and muttered:

"If I only knew — if I only knew."

And he did not look up until he reached the door of his hotel.

III

The next morning was wet; and the Count felt more disconsolate than ever as he gazed out of his sitting-room upon the little garden of his hotel, and heard the stems of the trees creak and groan as they were bowed down by a strong wind.

Ill luck had now pursued him at the tables for three days running, and he was rapidly approaching one of those crises to which his incontinent manner of life drove him from time to time. The absence of Miss Rayner added to his dissatisfaction. He was haunted by the reflection that, had he only summoned to his aid the necessary courage, she might have shown him a way out of all his difficulties. The suddenness of her departure had upset him. Before he had had time to realise

4

what it would mean to him, she was gone. In fact, Mrs. Rayner's tactics had been just a little too precipitate to meet with success.

The Count flitted idly from newspaper to newspaper, and smoked a cigar while he meditated over the situation. His mind was, however, too inactive to pursue an exhaustive process of reasoning, and before long found relief in a racing paragraph in the " New York Herald." He glanced quickly over it, rang the bell, and gave the servant a telegram in which were directions to put a hundred francs for him on " Sardanapalus," — fifty for a place and fifty to win. Then he took déjeuner in his room, lit a fresh cigar, and fell asleep.

He dreamed that he was in the gambling-room of the Casino, and that he was losing again time after time, and the croupier was raking in the gold in little heaps in front of him. The usual crowd of faces was round the table ; but one motionless figure sat apart from the rest, the figure of a little old man with a queer, triangular face: and he seemed very unreal and strange. Sometimes he would grow quite tiny, and his hands, which were folded in front of him on the table, looked like the claws of a chicken. Nobody but Dornstein appeared to notice him. And then he thought he heard Cecilia singing in the next room, and he left the tables; but he heard the flapping of wings behind him, and when he reached Cecilia, the little man was seated on the top of the upright piano. He was not more than an inch high. Now he looked like a little old man, and now he blinked with his eyes and held his tiny head on one side and shook himself just like a bird, and Cecilia laughed and nodded at him as she sang.

A sunbeam fell upon his face — and the Count awoke. A bevy of pigeons crossed the window, cooing and making a rushing sound with their wings. The clouds had cleared away, leaving a mild blue sky in which the sun was shining lazily, and the leaves of the trees, wet with the morning rain, looked greener than ever. The Count yawned, stretched himself, and after bathing his face in Eau de Cologne and water, strolled round to the Casino, the gardens of which began to fill with people eager for fresh air and gossip after the dulness of the morning.

Pezarin was just coming out of the gambling rooms when he met Dornstein, who yielded pretty easily to the Prince's entreaty to walk with him, instead of throwing more money away in that infernal place. The Prince himself had just lost, which had put him in a bad temper, although his fortune was large enough for it not to hurt him. He did not gamble regularly, but only in fits and starts, when he found nothing more amusing to do; and when he lost, however small the sum might be, it always annoyed him. He was glad of a companion at the present moment, and the two walked along arm in arm, discussing systems and theories of numbers, and telling miraculous stories illustrating the chances in rouge et noir.

"Why not dine with me to-night?" said the Prince, in a pause in the conversation, before Dornstein could weary him with another of *his* stories. "Afterwards we go to hear Coralie in 'Madame Perpignan.' Do you know it? Ah! c'est très drôle, and the music charming." His small sharp eyes began to twinkle as he hummed a refrain from the operette. Dornstein accepted the invitation with great pleasure; and the Prince, having secured the helm of the conversation, directed it as he pleased.

Meanwhile, considerable excitement prevailed in Lady Killigrew's circle; for some one had discovered, through Miss Savory, who had been at the station to see the Rayners off, that their boxes were labelled Paris, a circumstance which gave rise to much astonishment and surmise. They could not be going to Glyon, that was quite certain. On the other hand, if they had been going to stay in Paris, it was more than probable that Mrs. Rayner would have mentioned it; for it would not have sounded at all unbecoming, and was quite a fashionable move. Some one maliciously suggested that the Rayners were gone straight to London *via Paris;* and this view was hailed with much satisfaction, though in order to prolong the discussion which was extremely diverting for every one, it was tacitly agreed not to adopt the version as final. However, a week later, Lady Killigrew, to whom Mrs. Rayner in a weak, unguarded moment had promised to write from Glyon, openly published the fact that she had received no letter; and the solution to the mystery could only be obtained by accepting the suggestion that had been so ingeniously made. But until Lady Killigrew settled the direction of public opinion by this announcement, the geographical whereabouts of the Rayners formed an undying source of conjecture, which was stimulated by the Prince, who made everybody envious by his brilliant and amusing suggestions. Lady Killigrew said mysteriously that they had gone East, but refused to enlighten the company any further for the present. The Prince elaborated her disclosure by declaring that Cecilia had gone into a Turkish harem, and that Mrs. Rayner was visiting the Pyramids, which had been the dream of her life. He drew a picture of the smiling mother on a camel in a desert. Everybody roared with laughter; but only Miss Savory could see through the mystery of Lady Killigrew's remark, which was an allusion to the constituency of Lady Bland's father in the East End of London. All of these remarks were of course confined strictly to Lady Killigrew's circle, which was small and carefully selected, and into which Count Dornstein was never allowed to penetrate, and Miss Savory only occasionally, when her intimacy with the Rayners enabled her to retail some delicious bit of scandal that could not be obtained otherwise.

Towards the close of the performance of " Madame Perpignan " Pezarin whispered to Dornstein :

" Shall we go behind ? "

" As you like," answered Dornstein, indifferently.

" Bah ! Coralie is too old. When she first came out she was adorable ; une véritable figure de Greuze. Now — " continued the Prince, with a note of despair in his voice and a wave of the hand. He left the sentence unfinished. His mind was wandering back to the time when he first saw the face of Coralie, laughing out of the branches of a stage tree in which she was perched with her legs crossed. How irresistibly funny she was as she burlesqued every angry movement of the betrayed husband underneath, and he flew into the most dramatic temper, and stamped furiously up and down the stage. She used to kiss her hand every night to the Prince, ten, perhaps fifteen — Heaven knows how many years ago! To-night she had not even noticed that he was in the audience, which perhaps contributed to his present indifference to her charms.

Dornstein led him to the terrace of the Casino, where they sat smoking and sipping liqueurs till late in the night.

The gardens were now empty, for every one had gone home to bed. Only here and there a fairy light glowed, green or red, from a flower bed or along a path; for the rest had burned to their sockets. A heap of green chairs was piled up along the terrace, where the two men sat alone. One by one, the lights inside the Casino were turned out.

" So Mademoiselle Rayner has left you ? " said the Prince.

" Or you ? " said Dornstein.

Cecilia

The Prince yawned a little. He did not care at all about Cecilia Rayner. A man who can have his pick of the prettiest singers and actresses in all the principal cities of Europe was not likely to lose his heart over a Cecilia. She amused him; that was all. And he liked to see her spreading for him the most elaborate nets, into which he was always pretending to have tumbled unawares; whilst in reality he continued to enjoy a condition of sound security, and derived an infinite amount of pleasure from watching the machinations of the diabolical little woman (*cette bichette diabolique* was what he used to call her). But he remembered the evening when, passing the open window of the concert, he had seen Dornstein and Cecilia together, and, impelled by an irresistible desire to aid in the development of a situation that might be immensely diverting, he looked steadily at the Count, and then said:

"You can marry that little Rayner if you

wish. Elle est éperdument amourachée de toi, mon cher."

Dornstein sighed. His losses weighed heavily upon him, and to get money he would have consented to marry a girl far less attractive than Miss Rayner. Besides, with Cecilia, you could do as you liked afterwards. She was enough of the world to know that men are wicked creatures, and not to set too high a store on the fidelity of a husband. And yet he was not quite certain of her. . . . There were times when she frightened him; and as for her mother, he had never quite forgotten the look that came into Mrs. Rayner's eyes (those eyes that were so clearly the eyes of Cecilia), when, in her presence, he had borrowed a hundred francs from the honourable Hubert. He had reproached himself very much for it afterwards. It was a cursed piece of folly to have exposed himself so gratuitously. But he bluffed it off the next morning, by declaring that he had won five hundred pounds with the honourable Hubert's lucky French note.

" She gave me her card to go and see her in London," he said at last. " If I thought I really had a chance, I would brave the sea and make a visit in the autumn — Ein hübsches Frauenzimmer," he muttered to himself, as he passed his hand nervously over his beard. The Prince here thought it wise to explain his own position in the matter.

" As for me, mon cher Dornstein, I tell you quite frankly, she flirted with me just out of play, because it amused her. That is her character. On one occasion, — yes, I do not mind telling you that on one occasion I reproached her with it," said Pezarin, with an air of importance.

" And her answer ? " asked Dornstein.

" She said that there was one person with whom she never amused herself. I said, ' I know him : his name is the Count Gustav Dornstein ; ' and she made no reply, but her face grew very red. She pretended to be quite offended with me. That was her character again. Ah! les femmes — les femmes," and this time the Prince sighed with the air of a man for whom all the illusions of life have passed away.

For a few moments there was silence.

" She must be terribly rich," said the Prince, blowing a cloud of smoke into the air, and following it with his eyes.

Dornstein jumped at once.

" If I thought —"

" My servant Nicholas has heard it. They say her jewels are magnificent; but she will not wear them here, because she does not wish to excite too much attention. And the house in London — a palace, mon cher: horses, carriages, receptions — enfin tout-à-fait high-life," and the Prince yawned again, as if for him " le high-life " was the dullest thing in the world.

Dornstein, who had by this time drunk many liqueurs, nearly wept at the Prince's description, and was seized with a generous affection for the nobility of his conduct, so that he grasped him by the hand and asked him anxiously, —

"But is it true — really true — not only babble?" At this the Prince took a very high tone, said he was not accustomed to have his honour doubted, and talked of meeting Herr Graf Gustav von Dornstein early in the morning before the town was awake, at the little beer garden at Keller's, on the outskirts of Emilienbad, where he could have every opportunity of learning whether the Prince was a man who spoke the truth, and meant what he said or not.

IV

THE view of the Rayners' destination which
was ultimately accepted in Emilienbad was justified by the facts. Much as Mrs. Rayner
objected to being in town earlier than at the
end of September, before which none of the
acquaintances whom she respected ever showed
their faces in a London street, this time her
resources had become so limited that no alter-
native was left. Accordingly, on a wet day at
the close of the first week in September, an
omnibus deposited Mrs. and Miss Rayner,
with their five large trunks, at their house in
the neighbourhood of Hyde Park.

It stood at the corner of two roads, and the
blackened yellow plaster of the front had
begun to peel, leaving large white scars, which
added to the sense of desolation which oppressed you when you approached it.

Cecilia

A porter from the omnibus jumped off as it stopped, and disappeared through the porch which led through a shallow strip of garden to the front door, on which was written in tall, discoloured letters " Davenport Lodge." The door did not open for some time, in spite of repeated knocks. At last it was pulled back very slightly, and a sallow face, with stunted black whiskers, peered at the porter, who pushed until a short man in ill-fitting, greasy dress clothes, with soiled linen, stood revealed before him.

" 'Urry up : it's the missus," said the porter. But the slovenly, sallow-faced man did not answer. He only sniggered and made his way slowly to the omnibus in which Mrs. Rayner was sitting as motionless as a statue, while her impatience was growing every minute. When at last the servant's face appeared at the window :

" Now then, Firewood," said Mrs. Rayner, majestically, " a little quicker, if you please."

Cecilia

He opened the door, and the two ladies stepped out, and Cecilia tripped in front of Mrs. Rayner through the porch to the front door, where she stood waiting in the rain until her mother joined her, and they both passed first into the hall and then upstairs into their bedrooms.

The inside of the house was even more depressing than the outside. The dinginess of the walls added to the darkness due to a scarcity of windows. Everything wore a faded, almost decayed look. This was especially noticeable in the drawing-room, which was at the back of the house. It was a long, narrow room crowded with knick-knacks. The walls were a faint grey colour from which the heads and bodies of unwashed cherubim occasionally emerged. Here and there, at broken intervals, fragments of floral wreaths were just discernible. The ceiling was a cloud of black dust. Opposite the door, which was at one end of the room, was a large bay-window, heavily draped with dusty, red damask curtains, so that very little light could penetrate.

The bay-window looked out upon what was known at Davenport Lodge as "the orchard," —a plot of ground overgrown with long grass and thick, rank weeds which had not been cut for years. At the bottom of this plot was a row of five stunted trees which were, no doubt, responsible for the name by which this waste land was known. You could not call it a garden; for it had none of the qualities usually associated with a garden. To have called it a field, would have been a reflection on the neighbourhood, so it was called an orchard; and Mrs. Rayner used to explain to her visitors how anxious she was to have it made into a neat, trim garden, but that her daughter would not hear of it. She would even quote the words in which Cecilia's objections were expressed: "But it is so pretty as it is, mamma, so wild, so romantic. You would spoil it, if you were to make it into a proper garden."

In the summer Cecilia would put on a white stuff dress and a large, yellow straw hat with long, yellow ribbons flowing from it, and give tea in the orchard to the visitors on her mother's day at home. She would also hand round a plate of apples, which were supposed to have been just plucked from the trees. Nobody ever took them; but they gave a decided flavour of romance to the scene.

And from year to year the grass grew longer and wilder. . . .

It had never been cut since the death of Gottfried Rehner, fifteen years ago. Mrs. Rayner seldom alluded to her deceased husband, but when compelled to do so always spoke of him as a kind of Emperor owning half India in rice plantations.

But the neighbourhood had its own version of the family history of the Rayners. Briefly, it was this.

Cecilia

Gottfried Rehner was a widower with three children when he married his governess, Miss Panton. He was a German who had come to England as a boy, and made a business by his own ability and exertion. He married at twenty-five, and ten years later his wife died. It was a loss to him which he never recovered. They lived happily together at Davenport Lodge; it was not called Davenport Lodge then; it was only twenty-two Tollerton Road, and Gottfried Rehner used to add Bayswater, by way of explanation, as indeed it was as much Bayswater as Hyde Park, being exactly on the border between the two.

When Mrs. Rehner died, Miss Panton, who was governess to her eldest child, proved of invaluable assistance to the broken-hearted widower. There was nothing which this accomplished and designing young lady did not do to lighten the burden of Mr. Rehner's loss, as far as was possible, until one day, in a fit of generous gratitude, he offered to marry her, just three years after the death of his first wife.

It had been a hard three years for Miss Panton, but she was kept up to her duty by the prospect of good fortune in the future; and her virtue and foresight met with their reward.

They lived together for seven years, and then he died, not altogether unshaken in his faith in his second wife; for, soon after they were married, she threw off the guise of humility, which had hitherto been her most powerful weapon, and showed some contempt for the simple manners and foreign pronunciation of her husband.

The bulk of his money was left to his first wife's children, who were entrusted to the care of a brother in Bombay,—a direction of which Mrs. Rayner appreciated the prudence far more than that which had prompted her husband to leave to her and Cecilia, the only child of the marriage, a very moderate sum of money and the house in Tollerton Road, which she declared she always disliked intensely.

The first thing that she did was to alter her name from Rehner to Rayner, alleging as her reason for the change that she was worried to death by the tradespeople, who never could spell the German name. Soon afterwards, she introduced the name of Davenport, which she asserted was her mother's family name, and had it printed on her cards; so that she was announced everywhere ·as Mrs. Davenport Rayner. Twenty-two Tollerton Road began to be alluded to as The Lodge, and then as Davenport Lodge, and by substituting the description "W" on her cards for Hyde Park, which she always called it, or Bays-water, as her husband had always called it, she avoided all controversy as to which of the two districts really included the house.

Having made these preliminary arrangements, she settled down to the education of Cecilia, whom she herself taught up to the age of twelve years, preferring to devote her time to the child, rather than to expend any money on the hiring of governesses. Cecilia, who had a natural aptitude for music, learned from her mother both to sing and to play the piano; and when she went to school, Mrs. Rayner helped her to prepare her French and German lessons.

They lived quietly enough in those days, for Mrs. Rayner was unable to pursue any social ambitions, owing to the age of her child. Her chief anxiety during that time was caused by the thought that the Rehners, her step-children, might at any moment come to England and spoil all her plans for the future. She never troubled to think out definitely in what way their presence would injure her; but she felt vaguely that they were better away. In the end, she was remarkably favoured by fortune in the matter, for two of the Rehners died of a fever, and the third never showed any intention of leaving India.

Cecilia

As soon as Cecilia was old enough, Mrs. Rayner started on a course of seasons at watering-places. All her ambitions were centred in her handsome daughter, whom she piloted from place to place, and whose beauty and accomplishments often procured for the mother an introduction to people which her own personal charms alone would have been insufficient to bring about.

For some little while after their return, Mrs. Rayner was in an irritable frame of mind. A lot of money had been spent, and apparently no results had been gained. Cecilia remained obstinately silent, and resisted all attempts to draw from her lips a confession of how she stood with the Count. The servants had grown insubordinate. They wanted more wages and less work. Mrs. Rayner treated every demand of this kind as a personal insult to herself, and made a scene whenever it was at all possible. Cecilia, with considerable address, managed to effect a compromise, to which her mother reluctantly submitted, though she protested all the time that it was equivalent to a defeat, and abused her daughter for her want of spirit. Domestic difficulties kept the two ladies occupied for nearly a fortnight, during which they did not stir out of doors.

V

LONDON was terribly dull; and it was quite exciting when one evening the postman delivered a letter bearing the post-mark of Emilienbad. Cecilia, when it was brought in, was seated at the piano, running her fingers listlessly over the keys; but her sharp eyes had detected the blue picture of an hotel on the back of the envelope, as the servant handed it to Mrs. Rayner. She continued to strum, while her mother drew a chair near the lamp on the piano, put on a pair of gold-rimmed pince-nez, and began to read the letter.

As she proceeded, she ejaculated "Cecilia! oh, Cecilia!" in an agitated voice every now and then; but Cecilia pretended not to hear, and appeared absorbed in a mazurka which she was improvising.

"Cecilia!" almost screamed Mrs. Rayner, at last, with a tone of command in her voice, at which her daughter stopped and looked up inquiringly.

" Read that ! " she went on, handing the girl the letter, and fanning herself nervously and ineffectually with the envelope, as she lay back in her chair, with anger and astonishment in her eyes.

Cecilia propped the letter up against the desk of the piano, and read as follows : —

HOTEL ZUM GOLDENEN PAPAGEI, EMILIENBAD.

20th September, 1886.

DEAR MRS. RAYNER, — I daresay you will have got to London by now. How naughty of you not to have written to us from Glyon. I am staying here another ten days to complete my cure. The pain in the leg is better, but still a great trial. Nearly every one is going this week. You remember Prince Pezarin. He took quite a fancy to me, and told me lots of things I ought to do to get my leg well. We used to walk up and down the gardens of the Casino after you left, and talk about the people. My dear, he is charming ; and he told me such a lot of interesting stories. One I *must* tell you. He says that

Cecilia

Count Dornstein has gambled away what little money he had, and that he even borrowed forty thousand francs from the Prince, which the Prince will never see again. He says that D—— has sold all his wardrobe to Jacob Samuelsohn, the curio dealer in the Genf Strasse, where we once saw that fine old Valenciennes, you remember. Perhaps when Cecilia hears this, she will not believe it; but the Prince is not a scandalous creature, and he told me particularly not to tell any one about it; so that he can have no interest himself in telling a poor old thing like me. But I never liked the look of that Dornstein. How are you, dear Mrs. Rayner? I hope to come and see you as soon as I am back, and want to hear a long account of your stay in Glyon.

Affectionately yours,

Herminia Savory.

Cecilia handed the letter back to her mother with a smile; but Mrs. Rayner's agitation was rapidly coming to a head.

"I told you at the time that your behaviour was rash," she said in an excited voice.

"Nothing has been done, mamma," answered

Cecilia

Cecilia, calmly. " He has n't proposed, — besides, suppose I love him, ought I to believe these idle stories ? "

" But he is penniless," shrieked Mrs. Rayner. " You cannot dream of marrying him. You would never have my consent. You would kill your mother, Cecilia; the child kill her mother. Oh, Cecilia," and she began to grow hysterical.

Cecilia tried to quiet her.

" I don't want to marry him, mamma," she said, " if you don't wish it."

" Wish it ? Wish it ? Do I wish my child ruined ? Married to a scamp without a penny ! Do I wish it ? Ungrateful child, is this all the thanks I get for protecting you ? "

" I can do without protection, mamma."

" If he calls, you must not see him," continued Mrs. Rayner, without noticing Cecilia's last remark. " Say you will not see him, Cecilia. He talked of coming to see us. Perhaps he is already in England. But we will be out when he comes, Cecilia. You must not expose yourself, my child."

"I can see him, mamma, without marrying him."

"No, you can't, you must n't, Cecilia. It would kill me. I could n't bear it."

She grew incoherent with frenzy, and then closed her eyes and fell back in her chair as if she had fainted. Cecilia rang the bell and ordered the Eau de Cologne to be brought. She sprinkled it on a handkerchief, and bathed her mother's face with it. At last Mrs. Rayner groaned and opened her eyes, closing them again instantly, as if stabbed by the sight of her ungrateful daughter. For half an hour she refused to move from her chair; and then she calmly accepted her daughter's arm and tottered up the stairs to bed, where she remained during two whole days and the greater part of the third, pleading a severe headache. During this time Cecilia directed the servants to keep the room dark and the house perfectly quiet. She herself undertook the duties of the household, and spent her spare time reading in the little study which was next to the drawing-room, and of which the windows looked out upon the orchard. The walls were covered with books and old prints, and over the mantelpiece was an oval photograph of the late Mr. Rehner.

On the afternoon of the second day during which Mrs. Rayner remained in bed, Cecilia, having inquired after her mother, and being informed that she was dozing, and did not wish to be disturbed, retired to this little room to spend the time quietly by herself. She was a little tired, and sat for some time in a low chair, lazily looking out of the window.

It was a mild day, and the sun shone peacefully on the waving grass outside, bathing it in a liquid light which mellowed as the afternoon advanced.

After sitting thus idly for some time, Cecilia

grew restless, and began to wander about the room. Somehow she was haunted by a vague impression of the time when her father was living. She could scarcely remember his face ; but this had been the room in which he had smoked and written his letters. She was so young (only seven) when he died, that she could not have known him well enough to miss him now ; but this afternoon she could not drive from her mind one of the few remembered scenes in which he had figured.

She was quite a little child then, and had been crying miserably over some lessons which she could not understand. Everybody had blamed or ridiculed her. She remembered now, how her father had come up to her as she sat at the nursery table with her copybook in front of her, upon which the tears were falling quickly from her hot, blinded eyes ; how he had put his hand upon her tiny shoulder, and comforted her, as he explained away her difficulties. A trifling incident, and she wondered why it had impressed itself so vividly on her memory. But this afternoon she could not shake it from her mind. She could almost feel the touch of his hand upon her shoulder. She glanced at the picture over the mantel-piece. Never before had it seemed so intimate to her.

She sat down again near the window, this time with a book in her hand which she had almost mechanically taken from the shelves, as she wandered aimlessly round the room.

As she opened it, she recognised her favourite "Esmond," and began turning over the leaves slowly, glancing down them as she went on. Beatrix was one of her pet heroines in fiction; and whilst she read, she would substitute her own personality for that of this dazzling beauty, in all the circumstances by which she is surrounded in the pages of the novel. Fascinated by the brilliant picture of the girl standing on the stairs in her scarlet stockings, with the silver clocks and her white satin

6

shoes, she used it almost unconsciously as a peg on which to hang her own personality, and, wrapped in a blind devotion for every detail of the behaviour of Beatrix, found in it an apology for everything in the actions of Cecilia which might otherwise have seemed to her without justification. For Esmond, she had no pity at all, and read with nothing but delight the story of his continual torture at the hands of Beatrix. She looked down upon him, considering him to be an insufferable prig. That was the impression the book had left on her years ago, when she had positively stamped with rage on reading the scene in which Esmond brings to Beatrix news of the death of the Duke of Hamilton.

As she turned over the leaves, she remembered how angry that scene had made her, and she began to search for it. When she found it, she was disappointed that it did not impress her nearly so much as when she had first read it. She saw a pencil mark against one passage, and could not imagine for what reason she had put it there, though she recognised it as her own. The words seemed to have no especial significance that could explain the mark.

So she read on to where Beatrix wants Esmond to take back the diamonds which he had given her on her engagement to the Duke of Hamilton, and Esmond makes a final appeal to the girl. And as Cecilia read the farewell speech of Beatrix, in which, in spite of herself, she confesses that she is sick and weary of the world, that Esmond is too good for her, that no man ever touched her heart, — the face of a boy rose before her, — a boy, fair and tall, with whom she used to play when she was a child. Edward Mason was the son of a friend of her father, and had been her companion and playmate, until one day, conquered by the beauty of the spring, as they were wandering down a country lane together, he had told her, quite innocently and simply, that he thought he was in love with her, and wondered whether she would ever be his wife. Something in his voice had told her, although she was only seventeen then, that he had stopped playing, that an impulse outside them had interrupted the game that they had kept up ever since they were quite little children. But she burst into a fit of hard, silvery laughter, and abused him, saying all the most cruel things that rose to her lips. And now, as she sat in her father's study thinking, the look of pain in the boy's face oppressed her. She had wounded him beyond recall. All that he had wanted was that she should be friendly. She might have laughed in such a way that he would have laughed with her; but she had heaped ridicule and contempt upon him. The coldness of her laughter had come upon him unawares and chilled him, so that he could never bear to see again the girl whose friendship he had valued too dearly, but in vain; for he realised that on her side it had been the result of early association and nothing more.

Cecilia

They had parted at the end of the lane. That was all. To-day Cecilia saw the scene as clearly as she had seen it five or six years ago. But to-day she saw also, that within its pale-green buds, within the faint mystery of colour in the sky overhead, within the liquid notes of the birds who sang as if played upon by the sun, that tiny road with its mantling hedges, clad in all the beauty of a perfect spring day, held in her remembrance a divine place, and represented the symbol of one beautiful thing that had passed close to her in her sordid life. The beauty of it had escaped her then; but now it emerged from the past and assailed her, making her desolate.

"The one bit of romance — the one bit of romance," she murmured, "and I threw it away."

The book slipped through her fingers into her lap, and she could only see a blurred mass of tangled green, that shook and quivered before her tearful eyes, as she gazed out of the window.

She tried to force her mind back to think of Beatrix.

" Her mother was good and gentle, like an angel," she murmured. " Mine —"

But the face of the boy whom she had so wantonly wounded still haunted her, throwing her back into the past, and again the presence of her father seemed to surround her. She fancied she saw a pained look in his eyes, as if he were unhappy at the sight of the corruption that had entered his house. She thought of her life, with its tawdry sordidness, of the great race for marriage to which her mother was ever urging her, the eternal whirl of pleasure, night after night, the violent brightness of the ball-room and the play-house, and then the dingy colour of the walls at home, the faded angels in the drawing-room, the discontent of the servants, the wrangling over a few paltry bones — Was this all that there was in life? This, the beginning and the end of all things? Her isolation was terrible. At that moment, if the boy whom she had scorned had stood before her, she would have clung to him and implored him to save her. But he was only one of the endless things that go to make up the impossibility of life. As a great light flashed suddenly on a dark and difficult way, and as suddenly withdrawn, so was the remembrance of his face to Cecilia. It left her dazed and conscience-stricken, groping blindly for a way through the darkness.

VI

MRS. RAYNER was sufficiently tired of staying
in bed on the next day to declare her intention
of getting up in the afternoon. She made no
more allusion to the cause of her sudden pros-
tration, and even suggested to Cecilia that they
should pay a call together at half-past four.

Miss Rayner was waiting, ready dressed, for
her mother in the drawing-room when Firewood opened the door and announced a visitor
in unintelligible terms. Cecilia was fastening
the last button of a long new suède glove
which she had fitted on her left hand, while the
right glove dangled from her wrist, upon which
she had quickly slipped it, without fitting the
upper part on to her hand. She was looking
intently at the button, which was more than
usually obstinate, so that when she heard the
door open and the indistinct murmur of the

servant, she paid no attention, thinking that he had come to tell her that her mother was ready, waiting for her in the hall.

When she looked up at last, Graf Dornstein stood before her. He made a low bow, as she offered him her ungloved hand, over which he stooped as if to kiss it; but she withdrew it quickly, and, breaking into a fit of her silvery laughter, cried:

"Well, Gust—, Count Dornstein, this is a surprise!" She had nearly called him Gustav, but checked herself in time to save the last syllable.

"How good of you to come and see us," she continued. The Count bowed.

"It was my promise, Miss Raynair," he said. "When I make a promise — " he left the sentence unfinished, as he pulled a scented silk handkerchief from his coat, crumpling it up, and then pulling it slowly, first through one hand, and then through the other, whilst he carelessly revealed a large monogram surmounted by a coronet embroidered in golden thread to the observant Cecilia.

She was all smiles. She bade him be seated.

"Let us talk about Emilienbad," she said. "What fun it was, and how miserable I was when we left! Oh, my dear Count, you cannot think how miserable! Mamma was so ill, too, and I had to nurse her all the way up to Paris."

The Count summoned to his face the most concerned expression, as Cecilia went on detailing her mother's indisposition, while she watched with infinite joy his growing discomfort, as she wandered further and further away from the subject which she knew he was burning to discuss. Then, when she had three times resisted his attempts to divert the course of the conversation to a more congenial topic, once by dropping her parasol, a second time by rising to ring for tea, and a third time by showing him the photograph of a pet actor which stood upon ·the piano, she suddenly turned to him, saying:

"Well? And the Prince? and Lady Killigrew? And dear, dear Emilienbad? What did you all do when we left?"

The Count rose at once to the occasion.

"A great deal happened, Mademoiselle, and in a short time too —" He paused a moment, then resumed:

"The morning after you left, there was a duel."

Cecilia positively screamed with delight.

"A duel?" she cried. "A duel?"

"A duel," reiterated the Count, impressively.

"But what about?"

"On your account," said the Count, looking very grave.

"A duel on my account?" said Cecilia, almost choking with laughter. "Who, who —" she could scarcely continue for laughter, "who fought this duel?"

The Count looked steadily at her, chasing the laughter from her face. He had drawn the silk handkerchief through his left hand, and now held it stretched between his two hands like a barrier, over which he looked at her and said:

" The Prince Pezarin was one of the principals."

" And the other?" she asked quickly.

The Count did not answer at once. He dropped his eyes upon the carpet, where he noticed that the white thread underneath had eaten away almost all of the fleur-de-lys pattern which must have once embellished it.

" I was the other," he said at last, and then he rose and walked towards the window.

As he looked at the rough, unkempt garden outside, he realised that the Prince must have lied to him; for certainly the Rayners were not wealthy, nor was this a palace. But he was desperately hard up. He had gambled away his last farthing; and, under circumstances like these, even the modest fortune of a Cecilia was not to be despised. It occurred to him

that the story of the duel would fascinate Miss
Rayner, and as it was not easy for any one to
disprove, it being supposed to have taken place
in the early morning, before any of the inhabitants of Emilienbad were abroad, he felt quite
safe in using this harmless little device to
improve his position with Cecilia. What could
be more effectual than to turn the threatened duel into a fascinating reality, and then,
when the girl's heart was touched by the
tragical story, to throw himself on her mercy
and ask her hand for the reward of his gallant
conduct?

Cecilia had immediately seen through this.
She never believed for a moment that Prince
Pezarin would have taken the trouble to fight
a duel for her sake, and she was perfectly
certain that Dornstein had not the courage
to fight a duel for anybody's sake. But
with the Count's presence, all her talents for
admirable dissembling revived. She seemed
once more to be in the atmosphere of Emilien-

bad, where for six consecutive weeks she was acting a play from morning to night.

When the Count asserted that he also had fought, Cecilia stopped suddenly in the midst of a fresh peal of laughter, and, putting her hands behind her head as she leaned back on the sofa, said in a changed voice:

"You fought, Count Dornstein, on my account? You — you?"

The Count was so satisfied with the change of tone in her voice, that he did not alter his position for fear that the slightest movement might mar his success. He only answered, as he still gazed out of the window:

"At four o'clock the next morning, Mademoiselle, in the little beer garden of Keller near the station."

"And what made you do this?" asked Cecilia, softly, while malicious laughter, unseen by the Count, danced in her eyes.

"The evening after you left, the Prince insulted your honour. We were sitting in the terrace of the Casino, after the people had all gone. I had asked him to drink wine with me. We began to talk about you." And the Count turned round to look at Cecilia, who sat with head bent forward, her arms encircling her knees, as Desdemona sat to Othello.

"And the Prince insulted your honour," continued Dornstein, his voice swelling with anger. "I threw the rest of my wine in his face. I saw it trickle down the front of his shirt," he went on, growing more and more circumstantial. "It looked like blood."

He paused to see what effect he had made; but Cecilia, unable to listen any longer with equanimity, had buried her head in her hands.

Dornstein approached her with a look of triumph in his eyes.

"I was wounded," he said, in a tragic voice.

She looked up, her eyes full of tears.

"Where?" she asked, hoping to discomfit him by the question.

He put his hand on his thigh, and groaned

slightly. Cecilia plunged her head again in her lap, her whole body convulsed.

"Miss Raynair, I have done this for you; for I love you." He drew a small white parcel from his pocket.

"Here is a small token of my love. I bought it for you in Emilienbad."

He was so affected that he laid it upon the piano, without saying any more about it. For the moment there was silence.

"Miss Raynair," he said suddenly, "will you be mine — Countess von Dornstein?"

It was no good acting any longer. Cecilia raised her head from her lap, shaking with laughter so intense that the tears rolled down her cheeks.

"You silly donkey," she cried, pointing at him with her right hand, from which the long suède glove dangled grotesquely, "do you think I believe you? I know it's all a story to catch me; and it was awfully good — upon my word, it was awfully good," and she burst again into a fit of inextinguishable laughter. "As good as a comedy of Molière," she went on. "Why, you rogue, you've gambled all your money away; you haven't a shirt to your back; and you ask me to marry you. Why, I would sooner marry my man-servant!" She burst again into laughter.

The face of Dornstein had grown livid. He took up his hat and stick.

"Don't go," cried Cecilia. "Don't go. My mother will be here in a moment. Why not make your proposal to her? Wouldn't she do as well?"

But when Cecilia managed to see out of her eyes, she found the room empty. Count Dornstein had fled; and the next moment the front door slammed so violently that the whole house shook to its foundations.

In his haste, the Count had forgotten to take with him the little white parcel which he had brought for Cecilia, and which lay on the piano, tastefully tied up in pale-blue ribbon.

Cecilia

When Cecilia opened it, she found, to her surprise, that it contained a bracelet which she had taken to the pawnbroker Samuelsohn, the day before they left Emilienbad, when Mrs. Rayner found that she was so short of money that it was necessary to pawn a trinket in order to be able to pay the last week's bill.

The Count had taken this in exchange for a number of scarf pins which he had in his possession, and which, after his losses at the tables, were the only means left to him of procuring a suitable present for the woman he had selected for the future Countess Dornstein.

VII

THE vicar of the parish in which the Rayners lived was an old friend of Cecilia's mother. He had watched her ever since she had gone to live with the Rehners, as Miss Panton. At that time he was tutor to a royal princess.

Shortly after Miss Panton's marriage, a scandal broke out, in which the vicar was a central figure. It was rumoured that the pupil had fallen in love with her handsome instructor, and the royal household was thrown into the greatest confusion at the discovery of the state of affairs. To this, was said to be due the divine's sudden departure, his subsequent promotion to the dignity of a Canon, and his unquestionable success among all ladies who imagined themselves to represent fashionable London.

But independently of this fortunate episode in his career, the vicar had decided claims to popularity; for, in spite of his being hard upon fifty, his tall figure remained erect, and his head was no less handsome now that it was covered with white hair, which swept into a long wave over his broad forehead, and became his laughing, clean-shaven face exceedingly well. Moreover, he was a prince among small talkers. Nor did these social qualities militate in the least against his success as a preacher; for the Lancaster Gate Church was fuller than ever when he delivered the sermon, and he was as much a favourite in the pulpit as in the drawing-room. Certainly, a few respectable men, angry at his success, stigmatised his infinitely amusing stories as low-minded; but their objections were of little weight against the fact that society wanted the vicar, that whatever the subject of these stories might be, they were told with inimitable grace, and that, for the rest, the ladies would pardon him any amount of freedom on account of his handsome appearance and easy address.

Cecilia

Finally, he had the tact not to put an end to his reason for existing by marrying; and by this means he contrived to maintain in society a perfectly secure position. His enemies whispered that in the impetuousness of his youth he had become entangled with a small farmer's daughter at Cambridge, which would account equally well for his remaining single; but no one troubled to ascertain the truth or want of truth in such suggestions, and they only served to thicken the atmosphere of notoriety which surrounded the vicar.

Months passed away, and still Cecilia remained unmarried. Mrs. Rayner grew very uneasy. Trip after trip to the Continent had been taken with no result. The most exquisite dresses had been bought for Cecilia, and no necessary expense had been spared to make her the most attractive girl in London; and still no suitable proposal seemed to be in sight.

The vicar was much concerned at the girl's

want of success, and had many a conversation about her with her mother. He took an interest in her future, and came across her frequently at the Sunday-school at which Cecilia taught, in obedience to her mother's wishes.

Another occasion on which Miss Rayner was brought more closely into relation with the vicar, was in connection with the charity play, which was performed for three nights running every winter, and in which the vicar took the liveliest interest.

The play selected for this year was "The True Lovers' Knot," in which, as usual, Cecilia was to occupy the stage for three-quarters of the performance with the good-looking Aubrey Melville, who was talked of by the neighbours as a likely husband for the talented young lady. As a matter of fact, no surmise could have been more idle; for the young man had no money at all, having quarrelled with his family, who would have no more to say to him when he finally

threw up the bar for the stage, — a course
of conduct to which he had been persuaded by
the frequent remark of his friends, that sometimes he forcibly reminded them of Beerbohm
Tree. He had already made sufficient progress in his career to be taken on as a super at
the St. James's Theatre; and all who knew him
had gone to the play to see him struggle at
the end of the second act in a crowd of insubordinate citizens who surged about the stage
for nearly twenty minutes, each man shouting
and trying to push in front of his neighbours.
Melville succeeded in getting quite in the front
rank, and shouted louder than anybody else,
so that his friends soon distinguished him, and
were kind enough to say that he performed
the small part that he was given with great
taste; but a member of the Parish Amateur
Dramatic Club who, had it not been for
Melville, would have played the first rôle
with Cecilia, in the parish play, declared
that Aubrey Melville had reached the zenith

of his career, for he would never do anything half so well as push in front of somebody else.

The Amateur Dramatic Club assembled one morning on the platform of the large, hollow-sounding Town Hall, to rehearse " The True Lovers' Knot." The room, as usual, showed the traces of parish festivities on the night before: placards pinned on the wall, adorned with the painting of impossible hands, and, " Refreshments this way," and the deserted, naked stalls of a fancy bazaar, from which a few soiled ribbons dangled disconsolately. Everybody had arrived excepting Cecilia; and after waiting about for some time, it was suggested that they should begin without her, as she was not required to appear for the first few pages of the play. The stage-manager quickly arranged the stage, using such furniture as was at his disposal for properties. The scene was supposed to represent a garden outside the Rose and Crown Inn. Tables and chairs were placed wherever trees or seats occurred in the scene, so that the performers should grow accustomed to the area over which it would be possible to walk. The garden path was indicated by a chalk line.

The play commenced with a short conversation between the host of the Inn and one of his guests, followed by a light love scene between the host's pretty daughter, Miss Betty, and the gay Dick Taverner (Mr. Aubrey Melville). Occasionally the total inadequacy of the stage properties, and their obvious incongruousness with the words spoken were the source of noisy interruption. Thus, when the rollicking Dick Taverner asked Miss Betty to come and sit with him under the cedar-tree, for which some one had facetiously substituted a flowerpot on a little round table, there was a burst of laughter from the wings, followed by the angry protest of the prompter, who shouted, at the top of his voice, that if everybody was going to play the fool, he was not going to waste his time any longer.

There was a pause, and then Mr. Melville began again. The part of Miss Betty was played by a stupid young lady who was decidedly plain-featured; and the people at the wings were consumed with secret laughter at the absurdity of Mr. Melville's address to her.

"My beautiful Betty, do you see the sun going down behind those hills?" said the young actor as he pointed to a placard on the walls of the hall on which was printed "Sandwiches" in large letters.

"Far behind that clump of trees — far, far away, lies my home, to which I will take you one day, my pretty wench, to be my —"

At this point in the play Cecilia was expected to appear as the lovely Catherine de Blair, and her opening speech was, of course, a torrent of abuse directed against the faithless Taverner.

As it happened, Cecilia appeared at the other

end of the hall in the very nick of time, and, catching up her cue at once, strode rapidly down the room, while she declaimed her part with the greatest emphasis.

"Faithless Taverner," she cried, as she leaped past the prompter upon the stage, "is it thus that you requite my tenderest vows of affection? So be it. Farewell. I leave you forever to pursue your career of evil with that — that — woman."

There was in her voice the double mock heroism of a high-falutin' part and a rehearsal. The others were awed into silence by the fascination of her presence, and the malicious laughter in her eyes. But when she continued her speech, with a sentence delivered with intense dramatic effect, but obviously outside the text of the play, their admiration turned to consternation.

"Never more will I weep in secret for the Dick Taverner that once held my heart. For early next week — " She stopped and strode up and down the stage, trespassing recklessly as she crossed the chalk line and disarranged the properties —

" Early next week, I leave for the South of France." At this announcement, every one was thrown into a state of the wildest agitation. The prompter shrugged his shoulders help-lessly. Aubrey Melville rose quickly, and asked Miss Rayner what she meant; while the rest of the company crowded round the girl to hear from her an explanation.

In the midst of all this confusion the vicar appeared on the scene; and he was at once implored to use his influence with Mrs. Rayner to persuade her to defer her departure until after the performance of the play.

Cecilia wanted the vicar to come round at once to see her mother; but he pleaded want of time, promising however to look in at Daven-port Lodge in the afternoon; but he feared that little could be done if Mrs. Rayner had made up her mind.

Cecilia

The company then broke up into little groups to discuss the situation, most of them disconsolately, though there were a few who had been discontented with the parts allotted to them, and were not sorry at the prospect of the performance being wrecked.

Aubrey Melville walked to the door of The Lodge with Cecilia, declaring that he absolutely refused to act the part with anybody else.

"My dear Aubrey, how can I help it?" she said, as she gave him her hand, and then vanished into the house.

In the afternoon, the vicar called as he had promised. Mrs. Rayner received him with great cordiality. He was always inexpressibly welcome at Davenport Lodge, and each visit that he paid was regarded by Cecilia's mother as a delicate attention to herself.

"My dear, dear Canon, this is too good of you," she said, as she advanced, smiling, to meet him. She asked him to come into the study, adding that, as an old friend, he would

109

forgive the untidiness of the room. She always asked him to the study. It was so much more friendly. Besides, Cecilia was in the drawing-room, and a tête-à-tête conversation would be impossible there.

The vicar found no difficulty in approaching the subject which he had come to discuss, for Mrs. Rayner plunged into it herself almost immediately.

"We are going to the Riviera," she said. "I cannot stand the London winter: it oppresses me too much." A vague look came into her eyes as she spoke.

The vicar was a little perplexed. It was a sudden move, an expensive journey. He came at once to the attack, and had just reached the name of Aubrey Melville in his expostulation, when Mrs. Rayner stopped him with a significant look in her eyes, as the servant entered with tea. She thrummed nervously with her fingers on the table until the girl was gone. As soon as the door was closed :

Cecilia

"I don't approve of Cecilia's behaviour with young Melville," she said, with a theatrical air. She loved to make a scene.

The vicar smiled, pleaded the youth of the parties, and, with a sigh, pushed a white lock of hair from his handsome forehead.

"Young people must be looked after," added Mrs. Rayner, positively. "Aubrey Melville is all very well — but he is a penniless young man. As a mother, I cannot encourage his advances to my daughter. I cannot do it. I cannot do it."

The vicar saw that Mrs. Rayner's mind was made up. To unmake it would have required considerable trouble. He would have had to give himself away more than was consistent with his dignity and his vanity. But he suspected a deeper reason for this sudden resolution than the fear felt by Mrs. Rayner that her daughter would compromise herself with Aubrey Melville. He felt his way carefully, suggested that it would be rather dull for

Mrs. Rayner with her daughter alone; but Mrs. Rayner upset this objection by pouring forth a list of people whom she knew to be going, and who would be excellent company.

The vicar brightened, and, looking up frankly at Mrs. Rayner, while his voice was a strange mixture of indifference and curiosity, he asked if the Sterns were there.

"Sterns, Sterns, which Sterns?" inquired Mrs. Rayner, with an air of mystery. With an explanatory wave of his large hand, he replied, "The David Sterns."

"Oh, perhaps," said Mrs. Rayner, evasively. At this moment Cecilia entered, and quickly gathered from the vicar's face that he had not succeeded in altering her mother's determination.

The vicar stayed for another quarter of an hour. Mrs. Rayner was delighted at the length of his visit, and even offered him a scarf to protect him from the cold, when he insisted on leaving. Whilst he was putting on his coat in the hall, she cried in an agitated voice to her daughter:

"Cecilia, did I shake the Canon by the hand? Or did I forget it? My dear, tell me, tell me!"

The words were spoken loud enough to reach the Canon's ear, as he took his hat from the stand, and caught sight of his own handsome face in a narrow strip of looking-glass.

A smile played round the corners of his lips as he closed the door gently behind him.

VIII

MRS. RAYNER's sudden determination was not made without good reason.

The scars in the plaster front of Davenport Lodge stared into the road whiter and whiter; the angels on the drawing-room walls were retreating further and further behind the veil of dirt and dust which crept over them; and the fleur-de-lys pattern of the carpet was rapidly being consumed by the white thread underneath. Discontent reigned among the servants; nor was it possible to check the evil rumours that they were spreading in the neighbourhood.

Mrs. Rayner felt that she was called upon to make one final effort. Foreign aristocrats had no money: that was the lesson the Dornstein episode had taught. Meanwhile, Aubrey

Cecilia

Melville was a source of considerable anxiety. Cecilia always concealed her inmost feelings in the presence of her mother, wrapping them round in a cold, unquestioning obedience to whatever was asked of her, whenever it was possible to comply. This made her mother all the more afraid that, at a moment when her daughter's pleasure was in her own hands, the girl would seize it without regard to the consequences; and the possibility of her eloping with the handsome, penniless, young Melville filled Mrs. Rayner with a growing terror.

One day, when Cecilia came unexpectedly into the room, she found her mother crying; and when the girl tried to console her, she only cried all the more, and asked to be left alone. As long as this woman was creating the circumstances round her by her own will, she did not stop to think at what cost she was pursuing her ambitions; but when circumstances grew too strong for her, when she had to give way before them, then she was oppressed with a sense of loneliness and desolation. She beat her hands helplessly, like a child whose house of bricks, built up with an infinity of care, is swept with one crash to the ground by the dress of the nurse brushing heedlessly past it.

"What use am I? What use?" she reflected bitterly. "I might as well go back to Exeter. No one would miss me. No one cares, not even Cecilia. I am getting old; I ought to die."

For a moment, she saw the cottage where she was born, with its tiny back-garden and the clothes-line stretched across it. She saw her father, seated as usual on the top of a projecting buttress of the house, painting a large canvas. She remembered the pattern of the dirty, slovenly dressing-gown in which he sat. Miss Savory's seminary, where for six months she had taught French when that institution was first opened, forced itself upon her mind. Through the thin wall which separated the two class-rooms, she could hear the droning of the girls and Herminia's voice as she dictated. But she quickly thrust the picture that was rising before her from her mind. She had cultivated the habit of forgetting this part of her life for about twenty years, and its intrusion now pained and discomfited her. As soon as the sting of her momentary isolation had passed from her, she began to turn her mind to more practical considerations.

She was turning out a cupboard in the study one afternoon, when she came across an old box which had been unopened for many years. It contained a quantity of knick-knacks,—a pipe of the late Mr. Rehner, a silver medal gained at an exhibition for "Rehner's Rice," bits of string, newspaper cuttings, and, at the bottom of all, a photograph, which Mrs. Rayner drew forth with some curiosity.

It was the portrait of a friend of Mr. Rehner, a Jew who had invented a patent coffee machine by means of which he had accumulated a very large fortune. Mrs. Rayner gazed at the faded picture for a moment, then let it drop into the box, and with an air of intelligent meditation sat down by the fire and began to think.

The Sterns lived a great deal abroad. No rumours of the tottering condition of Davenport Lodge would probably have reached them. The two sons, though educated in England, came of German parents. There was no denying that, nor that their manners and appearance were not as distinguished as Mrs. Rayner would have liked. But distinction was less indispensable than the security which money could give, and the more practical side of the question was growing daily in importance. A visit to the Riviera would be well timed. At all events, it would be the means of averting the danger likely to be run if the parish play were to be performed. The only difficulty was how to obtain money enough for so expensive a journey.

Mrs. Rayner was about to abandon the whole enterprise as hopeless on this account, when she suddenly remembered that, locked up in a safe at the bank, were a few pieces of silver which had been left to her by her husband. She had never used them in the house, for many reasons, chiefly because they would have given the servants a false impression of her wealth, and she would have had to pay them higher wages. She had not, however, parted with them; because she hoped one day to bring them forth as old family relics that had descended from generation to generation for more than a century. It was hard to give them up; but it was the only possible solution to her difficulty. The details of how a transaction could be effected were still a subject of grave consideration, and Mrs. Rayner was compelled reluctantly to admit to herself that it would not be wise to act without advice.

Cecilia

The only person she could think of as likely to be of any use in such a delicate matter was Miss Savory, who had known her as a girl, when they had both gone together to the same school in Devonshire. The friendship between the two ladies was kept up with more persistence perhaps by Miss Savory than by Mrs. Rayner, who always pleaded the distance when Miss Savory complained that she did not come to see her more often. However, when Miss Savory came to Davenport Lodge, Mrs. Rayner was always glad to see her; for although she disliked arousing the memory of early associations, Herminia had become a habit with her, and without being reminded of the time when their friendship was first contracted, she felt a peculiar comfort in her presence. Moreover, whenever anybody happened to be at the Rayners' when Miss Savory called, the old lady acquitted herself very creditably in conversation, was always abreast with the newest fashion, and was a decidedly useful person in a room, as she was garrulous and always kept the ball rolling. Other people had a cat or a dog to provide conversation for awkward gaps on "at home" days. Mrs. Rayner was fortunate enough to have an able substitute in her Savory.

She accordingly determined to consult her friend as to the best means of disposing of her old silver. There was no need to reveal to her more of her intentions than was absolutely necessary to secure advice. She drove one morning in a four-wheeled cab to the bank, took out her silver, and then went straight on to Miss Savory's flat in West Kensington.

Miss Savory happened to be looking out of the window, and was very astonished when she saw Mrs. Rayner step out of the cab with a wooden box. There was some altercation with the cabman about the fare, and Miss Savory, observing that it was not likely to be settled immediately, took advantage of the time gained

to tidy up a few things in her room. She
would have liked to have changed her dress,
but feared to be interrupted in the process by
the arrival of Mrs. Rayner.

In about ten minutes, just as she was taking up the newspaper to pretend to read, Mrs.
Rayner was shown in, and Miss Savory flung
the paper aside with the gesture of one who
has just read to the end of a column.

Mrs. Rayner put down her box, and at once
explained the object of her visit; for it was
no good to pretend to have come to see her
Savory and nothing more.

"With you, Herminia, I think I can be
perfectly frank. The fact is, I want to go
away, my dear. Cecilia is a great trouble. I
don't like young Melville. I consider him a
very dangerous young man. You know what
I mean. But our expenses have been so heavy
lately, that unless I can make some money by
selling these old silver things, I don't know
how I am to do it. I have brought them for

you to look at. Perhaps you know some one who could sell them for me, and get a good price. I don't like parting with them; but what am I to do?"

Miss Savory was much flattered by this frankness. She took the silver from the box, carefully examined it, and was so lost in admiration at the workmanship and the shape of the pieces, over which she clucked as she bent over them, that Mrs. Rayner was at last obliged to remind her of the purpose for which she had brought them.

"Do you think you know any one who could dispose of them quietly? Of course I don't want it known. You can believe that it is hard enough to have to let it go without — without —"

Mrs. Rayner did not finish her sentence, and Miss Savory, interrupting her with "Oh, perfectly so, perfectly so," paused in her scrutiny of a filigree basket which she was holding up to the light.

"Perhaps the Colonel," she said at last, "might be able to help us."

"Ah! the Colonel," said Mrs. Rayner, a little disappointed. The Colonel was rather a standing joke; for Miss Savory never appeared anywhere without introducing him into the conversation two or three times.

"He has a very large circle of influential friends," continued Miss Savory, pompously. "Perhaps he will be coming in to-night to play over the Gavotte with me, and then I will ask him."

Mrs. Rayner was rather disheartened. She had not much faith in the Colonel; but she was obliged to acquiesce in Miss Savory's suggestion, for fear of offending her and ruining her chances altogether. So it was agreed that Miss Savory, as soon as she had an offer, should communicate it to Mrs. Rayner, who shortly afterwards took her leave, not without considerable misgiving as to the ultimate success of her visit.

Cecilia

Only three days afterwards, however, she received a note from Miss Savory containing an offer of one hundred and thirty pounds, which she promptly accepted, preferring the certainty of receiving the money to the possibility of the whole transaction falling to the ground, if she were to waste time by investigating it more closely. It was more money than she had expected to raise, and it served her purpose in enabling her to go away immediately.

Having taken precautions of this kind, it was not surprising that the vicar's rather half-hearted attempt to keep her longer in London had failed; and, in less than a week after his visit, the mother and daughter were on their way to Cannes. Cecilia obeyed as usual, without a further protest than that to which she had urged the vicar in her own behalf.

IX

As the mother and daughter glided along the beautiful coast in the early morning, Mrs. Rayner was lost in admiration at every fresh turn of the landscape. She had never been to the Riviera before, and was experiencing for the first time the luxury of warm air and a brilliant sky in midwinter. She was intoxicated by the smell of the flowers which floated through the open window as the train rushed along; and the houses — a dazzling white under the morning sun — filled her with wonder and delight.

She forgot everything but the physical joy with which the scenery inspired her, and cried out repeatedly:

" How lovely! Cecilia, look, look, my dear, at the roses — geranium."

But Cecilia sat back in the carriage, paying but little heed to her mother's enthusiasm.

Cecilia

The beauty of the scene affected her too; but it made her bitter and cynical. She was wondering for what reason she had been brought here. She guessed that some sordid motive had prompted her mother's sudden departure, and her knowledge of the truth seemed, as they whirled along, to stain for her the beauty of every flower, to dye the sunlight and make it hideous. Always the same — always the same. And the beauty of the place seemed to accentuate the meanness of the world. In Emilienbad, when she had wandered along the alley of limes in the early morning, the same thought had once oppressed her as she looked at the crowd of corrupt, world-stained men and women, as they moved in their framework of green leaves that quivered, heavy with the morning dew.

Here, too, nature was scattering her gorgeous bounty broadcast: in the deep-blue water of the Mediterranean, in the colours and perfume of the flowers, in the steady brilliance of the sun.

Cecilia

Cecilia reflected, with a queer feeling of regret, that people had no right to be in such a place. For the world of men and women was bad, self-seeking. She too was bad, because she was part of the world; and to seriously think of rebelling against the lessons it taught would be childish, impracticable. What did it all matter? You cannot alter yourself, at least you cannot alter your surroundings. But at moments like this she vaguely dreamed of a set of people, perhaps of one ideal person, who might be cast in a different mould to that from which sprang the people with whom she had been thrown into contact.

As she grew older, she began more and more to consider such thoughts as an idle indulgence of her imagination; were not such things outside the reality of existence?

One evening in Emilienbad, when she had been wilder than ever at the Casino, and had felt an inward shame that she could not have expressed in words, her mother, who was more than usually pleased with her behaviour, looked proudly at her as they sat in their bedroom, talking and undressing, and then — kissed her. She never forgot that kiss. It was the turning point in her criticism of herself. Under it, the self-contempt with which her conduct on that evening had filled her had turned to a bitter cynicism. For a moment she was almost stifled at the thought of what that kiss might have been. Then all the harder side of her nature rose and swept everything before it, twisting her reason into obedience to her surroundings, so that she persuaded herself that she, too, was a hard, worldly person, just as heartless as the rest of the world, and just as capable of playing a hard game.

Only at times she was betrayed into a feeling of regret, and the gulf between her and her mother seemed wider than ever. Mrs. Rayner, too, had her moments of remorse; but they never happened at the same time as her daughter's, nor were they so frequent, for she had lived longer, and was less easily moved to criticise herself.

So the mother and daughter sat opposite each other in the carriage, while their thoughts were travelling in different worlds as they glided noiselessly into the Cannes station.

The platform was full of men and women, in summer costume, who had come to meet their friends. When the train stopped, Mrs. Rayner and Cecilia stepped out, bewildered by the strangeness of the scene.

There was none of the bustle which is always associated with railway stations in large towns: only the babble of voices, and a brilliant mass of colours, — the blue sky, the white stone of the platform, the hard brightness of the ladies' sunshades.

A butterfly fluttered over a lattice from which hung heavy trails of heliotrope in full bloom. And further along, the engine steamed lazily, the vapour rising from the funnel in a broad stream which quivered in the sunlight.

Part II

I

THE Villa Penumbra was perched on a hill far out of the town.

A broad flight of shallow marble steps, bordered on each side by a row of cypress-trees, ran up the middle of the gardens, which sloped to the brow of the hill behind the house for nearly a quarter of a mile. At the top of this avenue of trees stood a colossal marble statue of Hercules, under a fanciful canopy, of which the façade was painted with an imitation of trees and sky.

At the base of the statue, on which the faint traces of huge letters spelling Ercole emerged through patches of damp and tufts of moss, a seat was so placed as to command a full view of the little bay which lay stretched

131

out below on the right, looking almost as if it were a drop-scene from some theatre, with its miniature cape surmounted at the point by a church not higher than your little finger.

At the bottom of the flight of steps close to the villa itself was a marble fountain surrounded by tesselated pavement, which was skirted on either side by a low, crescent-shaped trellis covered with creeping plants and flowers: ivy, rose bushes, smilax: a profusion of coloured blossoms and green leaves.

The bowl of the fountain gleamed when the sun fell upon a swarm of goldfish who lay motionless just below the surface of the water.

The seat beneath the Ercole was the favourite spot of Albert Stern. Here he used to come when he was in a more than usually melancholy frame of mind, and he would sit for hours in the hot sun, his eyes half closed, while he breathed the perfume of the flowers round him. Sometimes he would take a volume of poetry with him, vaguely intending to read; but often the book remained beside him on the seat, untouched.

If ever he looked at the pages, the rhythm of the verse alone entered into him, — only the music of the words of which at least half the meaning evaded him. And when he read, his attention was diverted by the slightest sound, — the noise of a distant cart, or the faint rush of wings as a bird flew from one tree to another.

From the earliest time that he could remember, he was crushed with that sense of the vanity of all things which is born in so many of the Jewish people. It had made him idle at Oxford, indifferent at the bar, to which he consented to be called only at the instance of his father, who, having acquired great wealth by means of his patent coffee machine, and expended as much as was possible in luxuries which it required the imagination of a Jew to invent, now dreamed fondly that his eldest son would realise all the political and social

133

[handwritten marginal notes:] the sense that we are going to die anyway creates a sense apathetic wisdom wealth etc. makes him idle at Oxford because he ou is vanity is not everything perhaps

[handwritten note at bottom:] assumed that Jews ideas can be authodox

the sense of the vanity of all things

the son is completely apathetic. and his father is perhaps stereotypically Jewish. a complete dicotomy.

Cecilia

ambitions for which, though he was unfitted for them himself, he had a secret and profound admiration.

But every instinct of Albert thwarted his father's ambitions; for he had none himself, and at the age of twenty-five he was still nursing a peculiar discontent and a melancholy indignation at being born into the world which at times almost amounted to a disease.

As he moved through the crowd of extravagantly dressed people who thronged the villa from time to time, he would gaze sadly at the satin panels in the walls, the expensive ornaments, the modern Neapolitan statues, the Academy pictures in bright gilt frames, and think to himself that he, too, was part of all this, — nothing more than a luxury in which his father had chosen to indulge himself, — and he would mutter half aloud, " What a pity I·am not more decorative ! "

He was very self-conscious, and knew that he was ugly, — a violent type of Judaism, a mark for the scorn of the Gentile, with his dark eyes, his sallow skin, and his black, curly hair.

His brother, who was three years younger, was robuster. He shared the optimistic temperament of his father, into whose business he had gone; and he was by far the more satisfactory of the two.

The business was a common ground between the father and son; and, though David Stern had ceased to take an active interest in it, he was never averse to discussing business projects, and showed a keen appreciation and sympathy for the young man's enterprise and ability.

Mrs. Stern had been a very pretty woman, and for no other reason had her husband fallen in love with her when she was Rachel Helmer, the daughter of the well-known Frankfort banker.

She had never quite forgiven her sons for not being daughters; for, as it was, she was crushed by the presence in the house of three men, part of whose creed it was to thank God that they were not born women. Of her two sons, she liked Albert the best, because he showed more sympathy and understanding for her when she was ill, which happened frequently.

With Albert, Cannes was a passion. He made out of it a world of his own, in which he was a king at whose feet all nature did homage. He used to wander about all day in the garden or by the sea.

Sometimes, as he walked along the paths that wound in and out of the flower-beds, he would pick up an insect tenderly from the ground, and let it creep off his fingers onto a flower by the way; and he would smile to himself at the thought that, may be, he had been the means of saving the little creature from being trodden to death.

The Rayners had been nearly a week at Cannes before they came across the Sterns.

Cecilia

During this time Mrs. Rayner informed herself of the situation of their villa, which was well known as one of the largest in Cannes. Everybody knew who they were, but none of Mrs. Rayner's own friends were on visiting terms with them, so that she could not hope for assistance from them ; and it was impossible to call without a preparatory meeting, as the two families had seen nothing of each other now for very many years.

However, Mrs. Rayner, accompanied by Cecilia, took a walk daily from ten to twelve on the esplanade, in the hope that her regularity and perseverance would ultimately be rewarded.

One morning, as they were about to turn off the paved road to go home to lunch, Mrs. Rayner, who had been looking long and intently to the extreme end of the esplanade, suggested to Cecilia that they should take one turn more, adding that the air was so lovely and the sun so warm that it was a pity to go indoors.

Cecilia

As they neared the other end of the promenade, a sailing boat glided upon the shore with a rasping sound, as the keel embedded itself in the sand. Two young men in white duck suits jumped out, and, after talking for a few moments to the old sailor in the boat, made their way towards the promenade.

Mrs. Rayner had timed her arrival admirably. She and her daughter came face to face with the two young men, as they lazily mounted the steps. Nothing could exceed the vigour of her surprise as she shook one of them warmly by the hand, and broke into a stream of words, half of which she drowned with laughter.

"Well, this is a surprise, Albert! Or I suppose I ought to call you Mr. Stern. Such a long time ago! But you have n't changed a bit!"

Then seeing that the two young men were a little embarrassed as they raised their hats:

"You don't recognise me," she went on, "Mrs. Rayner, who knew you when you were quite tiny — dressed in white clothes then — but it's a long time ago."

At the sound of the name the young men were re-assured. They had heard it often mentioned at home, and could even faintly remember having met the family many years ago in Emilienbad, when Mr. Rehner was alive.

Albert began to talk of their boat; they always spent the morning on the water, and never came back till it was time to lunch.

Mrs. Rayner introduced her daughter effusively.

"Of course you know my daughter? — Cecilia, of course you know Mr. Stern."

Cecilia bowed very slightly, and smiled without advancing.

The younger brother, who stood a little way off as Mrs. Rayner did not seem to recognise him, looked at his watch, and Mrs. Rayner, observing his impatience, said:

"I mustn't keep you now. It's lunch

time. Come and see me soon. We are always at home on Thursday; and don't forget to give my love to your mother and father."

The young men raised their hats and hurried off, making their way through the town with the ease of people who knew every stone of the ground.

"What a pretty girl Cissy Rayner has grown," said Albert, after a few minutes.

His brother acquiesced with a smile which indicated that the same thought had passed through his mind at the same moment.

The mother and daughter returned to their hotel. Mrs. Rayner babbled all the way about the Sterns.

"Such old friends, such dear old friends! And to think of meeting so suddenly here!"

"The one you called Albert is very ugly, mamma," said Cecilia.

"Ugly? Ugly? Cecilia, how can you be so unkind? Certainly it is a matter of taste.

But I thought he looked quite charming in his boating costume."

"He is so Jewish-looking, mamma. And didn't you hear how he spoke through his nose? Of course he cannot help it," she added generously.

"I did not hear it at all," said Mrs. Rayner, calmly; "but if you tell me that the younger brother is the more attractive of the two to look at, I can agree with you."

However, Cecilia refused to compromise herself, and remained silent; and her mother did not press her, for fear that she might betray an undue interest in these young men, which might prejudice them in the eyes of her daughter.

A week later, Albert Stern called at the Rayners' hotel. Mrs. Rayner was out, and Cecilia had to receive him alone.

"Is this your first visit to Cannes, Miss Rayner?" he asked.

"Yes."

Cecilia

"And what do you think of it?"

"I think it the loveliest place I have seen," said Cecilia, enthusiastically. "You know it very well, I suppose?"

"I look upon it as my home. We spend nearly six months in every year here. It is the only time that I really live. I adore it for a hundred reasons, chiefly, perhaps, because one can be in the open air all day."

"That is a great attraction."

"To me it is everything, because I do not care for society. Of course for you it is quite different. You can enjoy dances and theatres and concerts; they always bore me."

"Certainly I enjoy all these things; but none of them are so satisfying as nature," said Cecilia, contemplatively.

"Ah — I see you understand — which is singular, Miss Rayner, for I have often said the same thing to people, and they have found it unintelligible."

"Oh, I adore nature more than anything!"

replied Cecilia, as if the subject were one on which she had made up her mind long ago.

" I remember going to Monte Carlo for the first time," continued Albert, " soon after we came here, and spending a whole evening at the Casino. I thought I had enjoyed it immensely, until I came out into the open air. It was a very beautiful night, and the sight of the sea, which was sparkling in the moonlight, made me feel that the inside of the place was sickening, revolting — What nonsense all this must sound to you," he said, interrupting himself.

" But I understand it so well," said Cecilia, eagerly.

There was a pause for a few moments. It struck Cecilia that there was a queer irony in Albert Stern, with his ugly face and awkward manners, expressing a sentiment which she too had felt keenly at certain moments, although, as she was growing older, the intervals between these moments were growing longer. Once that sentiment had appeared serious to her; now the theatrical side of it turned uppermost in her mind, and she gave a slightly ridiculous turn to the conversation, by applying Albert's remark literally to the present situation.

"I don't know why we are sitting now in this hot room," she said, "instead of walking in the open air. Wouldn't it be much pleasanter?"

He acquiesced, and they sauntered into the garden, making their way instinctively to a shady seat at the further end of the lawn.

"This is perfect," murmured Albert. "You must come soon to our villa, and I will show you our garden. It is the most beautiful in Cannes."

"I should love to see it."

They sat for some time talking trivialities to which the beauty of the scene and the warmth of the sun upon the lawn in front of them lent a peculiar charm.

Cecilia

It was late in the afternoon, and a multitude of brilliant colours began to fill the sky, clothing the large isolated clouds in swiftly changing costumes which waved and floated into countless shapes, as the wind played with them.

"What a wonderful sunset!" said Cecilia, looking up.

There was a pause of a few minutes, after which Albert whispered to himself:

"As if the celestial paint-box had been upset, and all the colours had run into each other."

"What a beautiful idea," murmured Cecilia.

"The sky is a fine palette for a painter," he added.

Cecilia laughed softly.

"You are a poet; so am I. I love to find pictures in the clouds. Do you see that tower of rose pink?" She pointed with her finger upwards.

"Yes. How exactly like a tower! And

now there is a man on a great horse galloping towards it."

" Where? "

" Don't you see? Quick! Look, or it will be gone before you find it!"

" I can see an immense horse — Yes, yes, now I see the man on his back. And do you see the clouds of smoke that are coming from the horse's nostrils?"

" Of course; he is a mediæval horse, Miss Rayner."

" How romantic!" And Cecilia clapped her hands in delight.

They went on for some time tracing the pictures that crept into being and faded away mysteriously before them.

Then suddenly it grew dark and quite cold. Before their vision appeared a pale crescent moon, within whose yellow rim a single star flickered faintly.

" It must be quite late," said Albert, hastily; and he rose to go.

Cecilia

"You must come and see us next Friday, when my mother will be at home. Good-bye."

And he hurried away, leaving Cecilia to wander slowly back to her hotel. When she entered the bedroom, she found her mother preparing to dress for dinner.

"What has become of you, Cecilia, all this time?" asked Mrs. Rayner.

"Mr. Stern called, and as he seemed to bore himself indoors, I walked him into the garden. He has just left after a visit of an hour and a half;" and Cecilia sighed, as if with relief at his departure.

"I met Mrs. Stern in the town," said Mrs. Rayner; "she told me that Albert had been here to call, and that his brother was in Nice staying with friends. He is to come back soon, and next week Mrs. Stern wants us to call at their villa."

Mrs. Rayner continued to pour forth all the details of how she had spent the afternoon, as she and Cecilia dressed for dinner, to which a gong, sounded on three different floors, summoned the two ladies as they were putting the finishing touches to their evening toilette.

Albert went to bed that night with the picture of the gigantic horse in the sky strongly present to his mind. He could not forget it; and it seemed to him as if it bore some connection with his life which he could not divine quite clearly. Obviously, the knight on the colossal horse, with whom he was only dimly conscious of identifying himself, was riding towards his lady-love in the rose-pink tower; but he reflected that it was curious that neither of them had observed a figure anywhere in the tower.

The night was hot, and he rose from his bed, pulled up the blind, and threw up the window, vaguely imagining that he would be able more easily to picture to himself the shape of the clouds as he had seen them, if he looked out on the sky, although it was now dark.

Immediately in front of him hung, low in the air, a large, luminous white cloud. Isolated amidst the clear, deep-blue sky with which it was surrounded, it hung partly over the villa, looking almost as if it were a concentrated mass of the clouds that had passed over head during the day, and were waiting for the first streak of dawn to disperse and spread its vapour once more over the whole surface of the sky.

Albert tried to see pictures in it; but he could not. Only it impressed him as something he had never seen before. And yet, he thought to himself, the tower and the horse are within its thick folds, and, smiling at his own fancy, he closed the window, jumped into bed, and fell asleep.

Meanwhile Cecilia, too, was musing over the pictures she had seen in the sky; and she began to laugh so much that she drew the bedclothes over her head to stifle the sound, for fear of

awakening her mother, who was sleeping peacefully at a few paces from her. She had recognised the awkward figure and the Jewish nose
of Albert Stern in the knight who had ridden
the gigantic horse, and she was filled with
inextinguishable merriment at the thought of
his riding towards the rose-pink tower, the
edges of which her fancy fringed with gold, like
the smouldering edge of a piece of paper which
has been lighted and then blown out.

· ··

II

CECILIA and Albert met several times on the promenade soon after the conversation in the garden of the Rayners' hotel. They always walked right to the end, away from the stream of people, and watched the play of light upon the bay.

"You must have a wonderful eye," said Albert; for Cecilia detected every minute a real or imaginary change of colour on the water. To which Miss Rayner replied:

"I never tire of watching the sea; I can look at it for hours together."

When the Rayners called at the Villa Penumbra, Montagu, the younger of the two brothers, had come back from Nice. He proposed to show them round the villa, while Albert whispered to Cecilia:

"Let me show you the garden; I hate all this;" and he waved his hand to indicate the innumerable objects with which the room was filled.

While Mrs. Rayner was raving over the Academy pictures and the snow-white marble groups (fresh from Naples) which reclined and languished all over the villa in impotent attitudes, accentuating by their whiteness the brilliance of the satin panels which formed their background, Albert and Cecilia wandered into the garden. But they had not taken many steps before it began to rain, and large dark spots fell on the path in which they stood.

When they reached the house, they found, in the sculpture gallery, a group of people, consisting of old Mr. Stern, his wife, Montagu, and Mrs. Rayner.

" How exquisite ! How wonderful !" exclaimed Cecilia's mother, as she leaned towards an inferior copy of Canova's Cupid and Psyche. " Cecilia, look at this exquisite marble !"

" Oh, mamma," said the girl, enthusiastically,

and Montagu began to point out several peculiarities in the work of Canova, whilst his eyes showed clearly that he was glad to be talking to Miss Rayner, and rejoiced that the rain had been the means of bringing the two back.

His father began to grow eloquent over his own possession; he was holding quite a little lecture, whilst his wife stood silently beside him, looking as if she had heard what he was saying a great many times before. Sometimes as he grew more emphatic, she assented nervously, saying " Yes, yes," quickly, as if to hurry him to the end.

The old man declared that the copy was better than the original, and emphasised his statement by laying a fat finger on the white marble. Then he closed one eye, retreated a little, and put his left hand to his forehead, making a kind of shutter with it in the manner of a sea-captain who looks along the horizon. Cecilia remarked how much he resembled

Albert when he did this; only the father was much shorter and stouter. But people shrink when they grow older, she reflected to herself; Albert will probably be the living image of his father when he has reached his age. And for a moment she forgot the villa and the marble group and the sound of the voices, and imagined herself in a room thirty or forty years hence, sitting in a chair opposite Albert. She pictured him wearing a red-silk skull cap, just like his father; the thick, greasy black curls straggled over the collar, and there were tiny specks of scurf upon the back of his coat, just as there were now upon that of David Stern's.

Cecilia was disturbed in the midst of her reverie by the voice of Montagu, who was asking her if she did not think the gallery would be a good place for a dance.

" I think it would be lovely," she answered.

" The statues would be very much in the way," objected Albert.

Cecilia

With some heat Montagu argued that such objections could only come from a man who was not a dancer: they would have a broad passage down the middle of the gallery, and the statues would afford opportunities for most exciting adventures in steering.

"In the midst of which," retorted Albert, "Cupid's wings would be broken, and the floor would be covered with marble fingers."

Montagu's lip curled contemptuously as he replied that so long as Albert would refrain from dancing there would be no danger; but old Stern intervened in support of Albert, and his brother's face expressed considerable annoyance that cold water had been thrown upon his suggestion. The silence that followed betrayed the disappointment of those who were anxious that a dance should be given. At last the practical mind of Mrs. Stern found a remedy, which she advanced rather timidly. She suggested that the statues should be protected by means of ropes stretched across the room.

The proposal was received with great approval; and Miss Rayner pleaded so prettily, that Mr. Stern went so far as to say he would see what could be done, and Albert, who felt that any further objections from him would appear too obviously selfish, remained silent.

The rain had now stopped, and Mrs. Rayner, who did not wish her first call to be unduly long, conveyed her intentions to Cecilia by a look; and the two ladies took their leave.

The brothers saw them out of the house. Then they wandered into the garden.

"She is perfectly charming," said the younger of the two, addressing himself to no one, but talking sufficiently loud to invite an answer from Albert, who offered none.

"Charming," he repeated contemplatively; but Albert continued to keep silence. In fact, he never mentioned Miss Rayner to any of his family, and only acquiesced, when his opinion was asked, in the opinions of the others. He could not bring himself to talk of her for many reasons, the only one of which he was at all conscious being that he did not know what to call her: "Miss Rayner" sounded cold, "Cecilia" affectionate, "Cecilia Rayner" too strange to escape the notice of the others.

His eyes were bent on the grass, fascinated by the drops of water that hung glistening on the blades, whilst at the back of his mind hovered that great picture in the sky into which new colours flowed every hour from his diseased imagination. He dreamed wildly of a happiness too intense to be intelligible to himself,—a phantom raised by a desire so strong that the possibility of its defeat could not be realised, and the expectation of its fulfilment could not be translated into words. To say to him that Cecilia was charming, was irrelevant, meaningless.

Cecilia

"You are not talkative this afternoon," said his brother at last, after repeated attempts to stimulate him into conversation; and he went into the villa to practise at billiards, whilst Albert continued to wander aimlessly over the wet grass, nursing his fancy until he saw in Cecilia a goddess spotlessly pure seated on a throne infinitely high, surrounded by rose-pink clouds through which a snow-white finger beckoned to him with divine grace.

When his father at last consented to give a dance in the sculpture gallery, it was a great triumph for Montagu. Though at the bottom of all he mistrusted Miss Rayner, yet his elder brother's tacit admiration for her was an incentive to him to endeavour to stand higher in her estimation than Albert. He had been piqued by the intimacy which had sprung up between the two during his short absence in Nice. Frequently they would talk and laugh in his presence over the rose-pink tower and the knight; sometimes they even began to speak a kind of sky language: all of which was quite unintelligible to Montagu, whose attempts to penetrate into the meaning of it were always successfully parried. At the ball, he would have the field to himself, for Albert never danced.

Everybody was enchanted with the arrangement of the sculpture gallery when the evening came. A canopy of very thin rose-coloured silk had been constructed, through which fell the electric light, shedding a soft, warm glow on the floor. The cords which were stretched down each side of the room were entwined with Nice roses and trails of smilax. The gallery was broken in the middle by two arms which turned the whole into the shape of a cross. In one of these arms the musicians were placed, whilst in the other, through which you entered the gallery, a small group of people stood or sat to watch the dancers.

Old Stern occasionally stole down from upstairs, carrying with him the heavy perfume of cigars; he just glanced for a moment or two at the dancers, and then vanished again into the more congenial atmosphere of the cardroom, in which a number of gentlemen were smoking, drinking, and gambling.

The company consisted of people of every nationality, who illustrated the cosmopolitan character of the Riviera by dancing in many different ways, to the infinite amusement of the spectators.

Cecilia danced every dance with the exception of two, during which she sat out with Albert.

"How well your brother dances!" she said to him, as Montagu passed them with a tall girl dressed in pale yellow, who looked right over his shoulder.

"Oh, Monty is a furious dancer, and he is very fond of Miss Delorme. There is no accounting for taste, is there?"

"But she is very pretty."

"That is the sum total of her virtues."

"You are hard."

"Perhaps; but I hate ornaments. Don't pretend not to agree with me."

"Oh, of course I agree. But your brother is entitled to think differently. We are not all made alike. For instance, your brother wears a buttonhole: you don't."

"A buttonhole is another ornament."

"You make me quite afraid. Instead of wearing this white satin, I ought to have come in a dark-blue, stuff dress with my hair parted down the middle, and drawn smoothly over my forehead, to please you."

"It would have been a pleasant relief in the midst of all this finery."

"Really, Mr. Stern," Cecilia remonstrated with a laugh, whilst she toyed with the flowers in her bodice.

"Seriously, you don't admire all this display, do you? Or, to put it in another way, you realise that there are things in the world better worth having than pretty dresses and big houses."

Cecilia

"How droll you are! But I object to the question. The conversation has wandered. I started with your brother, who, I repeat, is a charming person and dances exquisitely."

"Monty is a very good fellow; I like him immensely; we are great friends."

"He is so good natured," murmured Cecilia.

"Very."

"So clever."

"Yes."

"And so fond of you."

"I think he is."

The dance had finished, and they watched the couples leave the room, until they were left sitting alone in the niche opposite the musicians.

"Yet Monty and I have not a single opinion in common," said Albert, returning to the subject.

"Naturally; you are both so entirely different."

"You think so?"

"Why, of course," she said, surprised at the question.

"In what do you suppose the difference exists?"

Cecilia was seized with a fit of laughter, in which she contrived to produce the musical effect of shakes and trills.

"What are you laughing at?" asked Albert, mystified and yet charmed.

"Such a very droll question! How can I answer it? I know you both so little."

"Not well enough to have formed an opinion?"

"Well—you must promise not to tell your brother."

"I promise."

Cecilia was again seized with laughter, with which she interspersed her next remark.

"Your brother," she said slowly, as if searching for the right words to express the distinction, whilst she looked at Albert's face to gather from it an approval of her judgment,—

163

" your brother is robuster — more active —
more capable of dealing with the world — but
sometimes, sometimes — it's no good, I can't
go on."

"Oh, you must now; you have promised."

" Sometimes he looks so funny that he makes
me laugh. Just now when he was dancing with
that tall Miss De — Miss De —"

" Miss Delorme," said Albert, coming to
her rescue over the name.

" That's it; Miss Delorme. He looked so
like a bird. But how wrong it is of me to tell
you. Only I couldn't help laughing. But,
seriously," she continued, " your brother acts
more and thinks less. I should say he is
more like your father, while you are the image
of your mother."

Albert smiled, and silence ensued.

" Your mother looks very pretty to-night,"
said Cecilia, catching sight of the hostess. She
was standing at the end of the room, looking
oppressed, as if her responsibilities on that

evening were too heavy to be borne with
impunity. In her eyes was that melancholy,
tired look which is the mark of strong physical
suffering.

The music began again; and Albert had no
time to say more, before his brother, with the
eagerness of a keen dancer, claimed Miss
Rayner.

" Let us begin at once, while the room is
empty," he said.

Albert watched them circling round, cutting
off portions of the marble statues from his
view as they passed in front of them. The
room began to fill, and he continued to look
at the crowd of circling figures, whose movements seemed to him to be emphasised by
the cold, passionless stare of the statues which
gazed down upon them.

Mrs. Rayner saw her daughter dance with
the younger Stern for the fourth time with the
very greatest satisfaction. Her eyes brightened each time that the two passed her.

Cecilia

" How well your son dances," she said to Mrs. Stern, who sat next to her.

A flickering smile passed across the mother's face, relieving for a moment the look of fatigue which it wore.

"You must be very tired," said Mrs. Rayner. " Everything is beautifully arranged; it must have given you a great deal of trouble. I suppose you have done everything yourself, as you have no daughter to help you; but it must be a consolation to you that everything has gone so well."

Montagu and Cecilia danced the last dance of the evening together, as the gentleman who had reserved the sixth "extra" on her programme had gone away before it was reached. They flew rapidly along the gallery, which was growing emptier every minute.

When the music stopped, Cecilia almost fell into a chair, and her partner seated himself beside her.

"How I love dancing!" she panted, as she

fanned herself vigorously; "there is nothing in the world like it. It is the only time during which one can fling one's conscience entirely to the winds."

She paused a moment, and bit the top of her fan.

"What is the good of conscience?" she added, half seriously, "it only gets in the way of pleasure. Your brother is too serious to dance; it's a pity. He misses the greatest pleasure in life."

Montagu was about to agree with her with some vehemence, when she added with a little sigh, "Yet perhaps he is right after all. We ought to be more serious."

But her partner looked boldly at her, and challenged her with being perfectly destitute of morals and absolutely free from all suspicion of a conscience.

"Mr. Stern," she protested, "your accusations are a little grave."

But he laughed at her frankly and aloud, throwing himself back in his chair.

Cecilia

She closed her fan with a snap and tapped his arm familiarly, while she frowned at him.

"You wicked creature, you don't know! How dare you!"

She stopped, and her face broke into a ripple of laughter as her mother advanced towards her to take her home. They passed through the hall into the cold night air.

The stars were growing pale in the sky. And as Cecilia stepped into the brougham after her mother, there clung to her mind the picture of the hall with the few remaining guests in their wraps crowding round Mrs. Stern to say good-bye. Old Stern was standing at the foot of the stairs, his red skull cap on his head, and the stump of a cigar between his fat fingers, while with his other hand he was making a gesture of indifference at his wife, who was glancing reproachfully at him for appearing with his cap on, and bringing the smell of his cigar into the hall.

III

ABOUT a week after the dance, Albert was sitting one afternoon in his favourite seat under the statue of the Ercole, at the top of that broad flight of marble steps which ran right up to the crest of the hill forming the gardens of the Villa Penumbra. He was watching the fishing smacks in the bay, which appeared to him like a swarm of brown moths as they hovered over the blue surface of the water.

A miniature town lay stretched out far below him, — a cluster of tiny white houses emerging through a network of cultivated hedges and terraces. Through the stillness of the air came the sound of reaping close at hand, the regular swish of the scythe as it swept along the ground. The sun beat upon him as he sat there, causing him to half close his eyes.

He was thinking of Cecilia; over and over

169

again he went through the mental exercise of deciding that, however fond he was of her, it was insane to imagine that she cared for him; but the conclusion of such reasoning left him exactly where he was before; it did not diminish his desire to possess her, or his anxiety to know if she would yield herself to him. Then he picked up a stone that lay at his feet, and threw it at a tree a couple of yards from him. If I hit, he imagined to himself, she cares for me; if I miss, there is an end to the whole matter. He threw three stones, one after the other, aiming carefully and hitting each time. Then he went on amusing himself in the same way through mere idleness, whilst at the back of his mind lurked the same thought each time that he threw a stone: If I miss, there is an end of the whole matter. When he had thrown more than three times, it was a superstition with him to throw nine times. When nine was safely passed, then twenty-seven had to be reached. The possibility of failing to hit increased as the multiple of three increased, giving a feverish interest to the last few throws of the series.

He had successfully passed twenty-four, when he heard footsteps coming towards him. The stones at his feet were now all used, so he hastily rose and fetched three from a path close to him. Then he seated himself, and had just hit the bark of the tree with the last one, when Montagu stood before him. He had come to tell him that they were having tea in the drawing-room, and that Miss Rayner was there too. He spoke of her as " Cecilia."

Something in the voice of his brother irritated Albert. Was it that he had called her Cecilia, a privilege which he did not allow himself when he was speaking of her, though he always thought of her by that name? He answered, a little coldly:

" Oh, is Miss Rayner there? Well, perhaps I will come," and he rose lazily and followed his brother down the sloping gardens with their patches of brilliant flowers. As he approached the villa, he could see through an open French window which looked out upon the lawn. The party were seated round the tea-table, in front of which the sun threw a sea of golden patches which swayed from side to side on the parquet floor. Cecilia was dressed in white; on her head she wore a deep yellow straw hat trimmed with poppies and corn-flowers. She was smiling her assent to some remark that Mrs. Stern had addressed to her; and Albert thought, as he entered the room, that she had never before looked so lovely.

Eight or nine people, all of whom had been at the dance, were seated round the table, which was covered with a silver tea-set and many dishes of cakes of all shapes and sizes.

When the two brothers entered through the French window, Mrs. Stern was looking restlessly round the table to see that every one's cup was full and every plate covered with cake.

Cecilia

Some one had just asked after Mr. Stern, and she had informed the company that her husband always took a long rest in the afternoon, which prevented his taking tea with them.

At that moment the door opened just sufficiently to allow a head to be put through, and every one recognised, under the red skull cap, the sleepy face of old Mr. Stern; but, before they could greet him, the head withdrew and the door closed quietly.

Mrs. Stern murmured something apologetic, half under her breath, and Cecilia with difficulty restrained a laugh, more particularly as she noticed that Montagu was watching her closely.

The apparition of the head seemed to disturb the tranquillity of the company, for the conversation, which until then flowed easily, owing to the common interest which every one felt in discussing the dance of the week before, suddenly dropped, and a chill came over every one, when somebody said, rather helplessly, in the midst of a dead silence:

Cecilia

" The floor was so good."

A vague murmur of assent followed this remark, and the author of it, a young man, feeling that no subsequent amount of brilliance, however great, could obliterate the recollection of such singular ineptitude, rose, pleading an engagement, and took his leave. His example was followed by the rest; and Cecilia was just about to secure the attention of Mrs. Stern to say good-bye to her, when Albert said:

" Don't hurry away. Won't you come and see my favourite haunt in the gardens? Unless you would rather not," he added, rather clumsily, noticing some hesitation in her face.

" Of course I should love to see it," replied Cecilia, graciously, " I was only a little afraid that I had been here long enough."

While Albert and Cecilia were talking, Montagu escorted a little party through the gardens to a gate which opened upon the road. On his way back to the villa he fancied he saw two bent figures crawling up the steps that led to the Ercole; but he hurried in as quickly as possible, for he had run out without a hat and the sun was beating mercilessly upon his head.

" So this is your favourite spot ? " said Cecilia, as she sank wearily into the seat at the base of the Ercole.

" Yes," said Albert, pushing off a book that lay there, and seating himself beside her.

" What is the book ? " she asked.

" Oh, it would not interest you. I have only been dipping into it."

" May I see ? "

" Certainly," and he picked it up and handed it to her.

" Poems ? " she said with a note of indignation in her voice. " Why should you say it would not interest me ? I love poetry."

" I did not think you ever read poetry, Miss Rayner."

" Never read poetry ? " Again the note of surprise. " Why, of course I do."

Cecilia

They discussed the poets for a little while.
For each one Cecilia professed an enthusiasm
at once vague and comprehensive. She allowed Albert to suggest the names, and then
she drowned them in a torrent of praise.
Once she was going to suggest " Laodamia,"
but in the middle of the word a sudden doubt
oppressed her as to the correct pronunciation
of the last syllable but one; to have mispro-
nounced it would have been to turn the feeling
which animated the conversation into ridicule,
so she stopped in the middle and said, as if
a sudden forgetfulness had seized her:

" How stupid of me — it has gone clean
out of my head ! " Albert guessed " Laodamīa,"
and Cecilia breathed a sigh of relief.

" Of course Laodamīa — however could I
forget ! " she said calmly, while she congratu-
lated herself inwardly on her discretion, for
she was certainly going to make both the last
two syllables short, when she was seized with
a merciful forgetfulness.

Cecilia

After this incident there was a pause, during which Albert gazed in his old way at the bay, where the fishing smacks still hovered over the water, which was alive with golden specks that crept and swarmed like ants in the sun.

"I think you have chosen the most beautiful spot in the garden," said Cecilia, at last. She was holding her open sunshade half in front of her so that the white silk arch cut into the blue sky and the bay, making them appear doubly brilliant to her.

Albert did not answer.

She began to turn over the leaves of the book which lay by her side.

"I don't think you can really like poetry," he said.

"Why?" she asked mournfully.

"Poetry is a consolation for the unhappy: a sop for the melancholy."

"Well?"

"Well?—And you? How can you need poetry to console you? I want these external beauties," — and he waved his hand in front of him, — " I want poems about nature, because I am a misanthrope. I hate people, because they don't care for me, and so I fly to this. But you — everybody worships you. Wherever you go you have a hundred admirers. You — you — you are happy."

"I happy?" she echoed mournfully, "happy? — happy?"

Certainly she was bound to say this, for it was exactly what was necessary to secure his further confidence. She knew that the moment had come, and it was of no good to shrink back, now that the goal was within sight. But as she spoke the words, they seemed to her to bear a different meaning to that which they implied when she had conceived them in her mind. Accidentally, they seemed to reveal a truth which lay hidden far behind all the sordidness of her conduct. For a moment she hated herself, and felt a strong desire to speak out, to tell the man beside her to what the sound of the words had opened her eyes, to throw off the cloak of hypocrisy under which they had stolen from her lips. But she had not the courage.

He was touched.

" Not happy ? Miss Rayner ? " he said, with a shade of incredulousness in his voice.

" Not happy ? " he repeated, this time with emotion. " You who are adored everywhere, who need only hold up your little finger to have whom you please at your feet."

" That's just what you think," she went on ; " you don't understand a woman. You think that all she wants is to be courted, to be fêted, to be run after, to be called good-looking. I have had all this and too much of it. But human sympathy — what have we to do with that ? We are only women, and have no right to that."

She was again struck with the truth of her own words. She scarcely knew whether she was sincere or not. But as she glanced up and

saw the face of Albert turned towards her, the
reality of the situation forced itself upon her.
How ugly he was!—his sallow skin and black
curly hair were an offence to her eyes. She
knew now that she had only been cheated for a
moment out of her rôle—that she had been
talking as she might have talked to some one
for whom, in those rare intervals of human
desolation which swept over her, she might
have felt a real affection. But one glance at
the man by her side banished the illusion.
She thought of the house at home, of her
mother's anxiety to see her married. She
saw crowds of carriages whirling along the park
in the summer season: that was her proper
place, the sphere of life in which she was
destined to move. Was there not a hard wisdom in reconciling herself to the circumstances,
the conditions in which she was placed?
Clearly, therein lay the art of life. It was
a very old truth: the world was a stage,
and you could only enjoy acting in it if you

knew your part and never faltered in it for a moment.

And as she gazed in front of her, the scene narrowed the significance of her thought down to a single visualised instance which confirmed and strengthened it beyond recall. What was all this but a play? The brilliant picture of the coast reminded her of a drop-scene in the drama at the St. James's Theatre in which young Melville had come on as a super.

Albert was in the midst of a torrent of words.

" So you too have felt the meaning of isolation — Has nobody really shown you human sympathy, you who want it so much? Who could suppose that I should be the first to tell you — to tell you that you have my sympathy. I want yours. I want it more than I can say. I have been lonely; I have hated people, because my regard was never worth anything to them; but now — Is it possible ? "

Cecilia

He took her hand, and looked appealingly at her. All the misery of his past existence came into his eyes as he asked her the question to which her answer might justify to him a life that hitherto he had accounted valueless.

She looked down, and her face was a little paler than usual as she answered:

"Yes, Albert. You can make the coveted Cecilia Rayner your wife."

The light suddenly left the water in the bay, and a light breeze sprang up.

Cecilia had a queer feeling of satisfaction that it was all over; and they walked arm in arm down the steps, pausing at the fountain, which was the first object that made them realise the suddenness with which their relation to each other had changed. Months seemed to have passed since they went to that fountain on their way to the seat under the Ercole. Yet it was only an hour ago.

The goldfish had sunk to the bottom of the marble bowl; but as they stood silently at its rim a single fish rose to the surface. His body was scarcely perceptible in the fading light of the day, but Cecilia saw his motionless head out of which a single circular eye gazed steadily, ironically she thought, at her.

That night, as she got into bed, she broke the news to her mother, who was already comfortably folded within the sheets.

" It 's done, mamma," she said.

" Which is it, Montagu or Albert? " replied Mrs. Rayner, vainly trying to conceal her agitation.

" Albert."

" No — Montagu," said Mrs. Rayner, half incredulous, half surprised.

" No, Albert," retorted Cecilia, flippantly, as she put out the light and closed her eyes very tight, as if to compel herself to sleep.

IV

ALBERT'S mother was more pleased at the engagement than his father, who, though perfectly irreligious in his habits of life, could not quite rid himself of that superstition against marriages outside the Faith which his early training in Frankfort had instilled into him. His wife, though her character and temperament were unquestionably the product of her race, was frankly unSemitic in her opinions, and indeed secretly believed herself to be a Christian, though, in deference to her husband, she did not openly profess her convictions. To her, therefore, Miss Rayner's religious beliefs were an additional subject for congratulation.

When Montagu was first informed of the engagement, he surprised himself in a blind feeling of resentment, for which he could not account, but which was of short duration, for, now that all rivalry between the two brothers was put an end to, he soon realised that for Cecilia herself his sentiments were those of indifference, so that he could consent to act as best man with a perfectly clear conscience.

The wedding was arranged for June, and the Rayners returned in March, accompanied by Albert Stern. But long before their arrival, Herminia Savory had spread the news in London. She had received a letter from Mrs. Rayner informing her of " the wonderful working of fate." " Who would have dreamed," so ran the letter, " that my dear Cecilia was to be the wife of such a very dear old friend of ours?"

The vicar smiled when he heard Miss Savory quote the passage; and Lady Killigrew was immensely diverted when she read an announcement of the engagement in a paragraph of the " Times," shortly after which the Rayners returned to Davenport Lodge.

Aubrey Melville called one afternoon, a few

days later, at about three o'clock. The sound of talking and the clatter of knives and forks reached him as he was shown through the hall into the drawing-room. He had not been there for many minutes before Cecilia rushed into the room. He was about to offer his excuses for having disturbed her from lunch; but as soon as she saw him she broke out with:

" How are you, Aubrey, — my dear Aubrey? This is good of you — to come so soon after you have heard the news. Is n't it wonderful? You *will* like him so; he is an angel, and I have known him ever since I was a child, and he's just the sweetest, kindest, dearest thing."

She emphasised each epithet with a fresh shake of his hand which she held in both of hers all the time she was making this speech.

Melville caught the tone of the conversation. He began to talk of Cannes.

" Is n't it romantic? " she replied, quickly, taking the words out of his mouth, and making him sit beside her on a sofa by the window. "Fancy, only a month or two ago I was here rehearsing for the T. K." This was what they called the True Lover's Knot. "Now I am here again, and it's no rehearsing this time."

She broke into a ripple of inextinguishable laughter, as if the humour of the situation had never struck her before. Some time elapsed before she mentioned the name of her future husband, for she felt instinctively that Aubrey would be inclined to laugh at it. But she slipped it in skilfully as soon as she saw her opportunity. She made him rise from the sofa, and danced round him singing:

"And we're going to live in Berkeley Square: Albert has bought a house already."

As it was the only suitable thing to do, Melville danced also, and they were both engaged in a very pretty figure, in which he held her hand high above the little round table near which they stood, with his head gallantly poised in her direction, when the rest of the luncheon party came in from the dining-room, and Mrs. Rayner broke into the family laughter, which was caught up in a chorus by the others, including Albert Stern, who came forward a little awkwardly, as if he did not quite understand, and was immediately intro-duced by Cecilia to Mr. Melville — her " old friend Aubrey."

Miss Savory, who was among the guests, and who never laughed, threw up her eyes, lowered her head, and substituted her customary noises, which seemed far more in harmony with her person than could have been any ordinary method of showing merriment.

Miss Rayner was more brilliant than ever; and Melville was quite surprised to find that more than an hour had passed before he rose to go. Mrs. Rayner implored him to stay and dine with them; but he pleaded an engage-ment of long standing which would prevent him from having that pleasure, and took his leave, amidst renewed thanks from Cecilia for having called so promptly to congratulate her, which, as a matter of fact, he had entirely omitted to do, nor had he come to Davenport Lodge with that intention. He had no feeling in the matter at all. Cecilia was no more to him than an excellent person to make love to on the stage. She knew how to act, and never spoiled the effect of his sentences and attitudes by the usual clumsiness of an amateur. That was all. He was a little anxious to see the man to whom she was engaged, and the appearance of Albert Stern more than satisfied his curiosity. "He has one of the worst figures," he muttered to himself as he left the house, "of any man I ever saw. He may be useful, but he certainly is n't ornamental. Not that it matters one way or the other." And then he dismissed the whole subject from his mind, and began to think about his costume in the play at the St. James's. "I was too heavily made up last night," he mumbled;

and he stopped at a hairdresser's shop to buy a particular ointment which he fancied. "One can't be too particular about these things," he went on, looking at himself in a looking-glass in the window for a few moments before he entered the shop. The old piece was still running at the St. James's, and he was still playing the part of an insubordinate citizen, to which he spared no effort to give a distinction which should mark him off from the rest of the insurgents, who were most of them paid two shillings a night, while there were two or three besides himself who regarded their present engagement as a stepping-stone to a performance of Hamlet, by which they were going to electrify London in the dim future.

"Poor Aubrey!" sighed Cecilia, when he had left them, "I don't know what will become of him. He thinks he'll make his fortune on the stage."

"Mr. Melville is a very rash young man,"

said Mrs. Rayner, majestically; "he sets too much value upon his personal appearance."

"He is certainly very handsome," said Albert.

Cecilia acquiesced, but added that you soon grew tired of a face which was so devoid of intellect, — a sentiment with which every one felt bound to agree, but which reduced the company to silence. At last Miss Savory whispered a question concerning the arrangements for the wedding in Mrs. Rayner's ear, and Cecilia's mother withdrew with the old lady to discuss a multitude of details out of the hearing of the others.

Mrs. Rayner was in a fever of excitement. She made a scene with every one who questioned her on the subject of the engagement. Her joy was boundless, inexpressible. She showed it by broken sentences, paroxysms of the Rayner laughter, inimitable postures. She indicated that her delight was tempered by a great regret that the young people had taken everything into their own hands; protested that she had been ill-used, ignored; that the mother's feelings had been set at naught. She would work herself into quite a fury of indignation, fighting with imaginary resistance of the most determined and wilful character, and then accepting her defeat with touching and cheerful humility.

"What can an old woman say — what can she do," she would ask with a sigh, "when the young people are so hot-headed?"

Meanwhile Davenport Lodge was in the hands of the decorators. The angels on the drawing-room walls were being restored to a perfect flesh-pink; they were beginning to glow with all the purity of their pristine nakedness, and the most enchanting clouds began to float over them in discreet fragments. The dull, greasy, red damask curtains were replaced by new silk hangings. The grass in the garden was at last cut and trimmed, and the outside of the house was repaired, so that the large white scars in the plaster disappeared behind a layer of thick brown paint.

About a hundred invitations to the wedding were issued on old English paper in silver type. At the top of the card, in each corner, was a crest. On the right hand was that of the Rayners, a woodcock passant sable guttée d'argent, claws or; and on the left was that of the Sterns, a star of twelve points argent between two elephants' trunks erect and reflexed quarterly, counterchanged of the first and sable. Many of those invited gave a careless prominence to this handsome piece of decoration amidst the less imposing array of cards which lined their mantel-shelves.

The vicar conducted the marriage ceremony on a brilliant afternoon at the Lancaster Gate Church, which was crammed with people, of whom half at least were Jews from Maida Vale, the neighbourhood in which was the Sterns' town house. They had not been much in it for some years now; but everybody knew all about them, and a marriage outside the race always provoked considerable curiosity, even when the parties were less well known than Cecilia and Albert Stern. Moreover, it reopened all the grievances between the Reform and the Orthodox synagogues, and was an opportunity for general conversation as to the importance of religious ceremonial, the difficulties of attending divine service on days when quotations were rising or falling at the rate of three or four pounds a minute, as to the comfort enjoyed by Christian people of religious inclination who had a day in the week when there was positively nothing else to do but to go to church, whilst the Orthodox community indulged in the flattering conviction that every fresh inter-marriage was an unmistakeable sign of the corruption to which the reform movement had already led. Roughly speaking, it was Maida Vale against Bayswater, a distinction based on a sound geographical principle; for the Reform synagogue was closer to Maida

Cecilia

Vale and the Orthodox synagogue closer to Bayswater; and as too much physical fatigue is an enemy to religious fervour, almost the first consideration was to have a place of worship within a quarter of an hour's walk.

Maida Vale then mustered in great force at Albert Stern's wedding; and never perhaps had the Lancaster Gate Church been so full of over-dressed women. Everywhere could be seen hats and dresses of the latest fashions, while the faces of the women who wore them expressed at once the sensual comfort of having rich clothes and the curiosity in the proceedings which the occasion called forth. Many of them arrived early to "get a good view."

A continuous buzz of conversation, interrupted by nods and smiles as fresh acquaintances passed into the church, was finally subdued by the arrival of the bride.

Cecilia was dressed in a white satin dress with a low neck and a long train. She wore in her hair a tiara of diamonds, the present of

Cecilia

David Stern. She looked very pale as she walked straight down the church, without turning her head to either side, while the people pushed forward in their pews to catch a good look at her, and then whispered in Anglo-German to their neighbours as soon as she had passed out of sight.

Her demeanour was faultless. She did not betray the least emotion, except in the voice in which she answered the questions of the vicar. That voice was clear and hard; but it sounded very small, and a little as if it had been wrung from her by a force superior to her own.

As the bride and bridegroom stood together by the altar, a broad beam of sunlight fell aslant upon them, and young Samuelsohn, who had secured a seat in the second row of the pews in the church, nudged his neighbour, Mr. Mark Isidore, who was present with his wife and two daughters, and whispered:

"What a contrast they are, eh? There's no mistaking where he comes from, is there?"

and he added a tag of Jiddish, at which the other laughed, while Mrs. Isidore frowned severely at her husband to express her disapproval of such behaviour in a church.

The vicar made an excellent little speech to the bride and bridegroom, of which he delivered himself much with the air of a fashionable dandy who removes his tall hat on entering a room.

After the register had been signed, the Wedding March was played with great effect, on the organ, while Cecilia and Albert Stern walked together down the centre of the church, and there was a repetition of the pushing and talking that had followed the bride's entry.

The crowd closed together from each side behind them, and the air was full of voices and the smell of perfumes and millinery.

" Eine wahre Synagoge — nicht? " whispered a lady to her neighbour, as she bowed to somebody whom she saw at some distance from her, and frowned and smiled at the same moment, as if to convey her delight at seeing her friend and the discomfort due to the heat and the crowd. "I think our People could make Minyan here," she went on to her companion, who was seized with a fit of laughter.

Many sighed with relief as they reached the open door and saw the leaves of the tall poplars trembling in the sunlight, and the rows of carriages, and the straggling line of idlers that hung round the church.

The reception at Davenport Lodge was very brilliant. Tents were set up in the garden, and music was provided by a Hungarian band in pale-blue uniform. People wandered in and out of the tents in which were served refreshments of all kinds, although it was four o'clock in the afternoon.

Great interest was manifested in David Stern, who looked like a patriarch who had stepped straight out of the pages of the Old Testament. He drank two glasses of champagne, and then complained a little of missing his afternoon sleep, but otherwise succeeded in averting the reproaches of his wife, whom he chaffed openly, so that she was completely disarmed.

To everybody's infinite delight, the vicar graced the company with his presence. He stood in a gallant attitude talking, now to Herminia Savory, who was becomingly attired in a simple dress of dark-purple velvet, now to Mrs. Sherbetter, a pretty little woman who had come out of curiosity all the way from Brighton to see the marriage, now to Aubrey Melville, whose cadaverous appearance indicated that his complexion was already beginning to pay the penalty of "making-up" every night.

A separate room in the house was devoted to the wedding presents, which were numerous, and not characterised by any peculiarity. Prominent among them was some old lace with which Mrs. Rayner presented her daughter, and to which she had attached a large ticket with the inscription, " To my dearest, dearest Cecilia — a token of love from your affection- ate mother."

The departure of the bride was a most affecting scene.   A crowd of people stood waiting in the hall into which the staircase led.   Albert appeared in a light-brown travel- ling suit which seemed to throw into yet stronger relief the Semitic character of his features, so that, for the first time during the day, he attracted universal attention.   But he did not command the curiosity of the crowd for long ; for Cecilia, as soon as her arrival had been duly heralded by the servants who car- ried down her boxes and put them in the four-wheeled cab, appeared at the top of the stairs, her head turned to speak some order to an invisible person on the upper landing. She was dressed in fawn and pale-blue cloth, and on her head she wore a large yellow straw hat trimmed with poppies.   She tripped lightly down the stairs, her face radiant with smiles.

Cecilia

A space was made for her in the crowd, into which Mrs. Rayner made her way. She threw herself into the most agonised poses, clasped her daughter, and embraced her ecstatically. This was perhaps the greatest — the most dramatic moment of her life, and she knew how to appreciate it.

"Good-bye, my child! my dear, my Cecilia!" she exclaimed, theatrically. "God bless you! God bless you!"

A hail-storm of rice was showered at the couple as they passed through the door, down the steps; and in a few minutes the cab drove off.

"Look at the white slipper!" said some one.

Everybody crowded onto the doorsteps, the rice making a queer grinding sound as they crushed it underfoot.

They saw the back of the cab, which was already some way down the road, and something white seemed to cling to one of the wheels as it went round.

Part III

I

DURING the whole of the summer of '87 Prince Pezarin was in the hands of the doctors. He had been looking forward to a very gay season at Ostende, where La Poussière, then at the height of her career at the Variétés in Paris, had promised to meet him; but the doctors prescribed rest and a minimum of excitement, and, when the Prince expostulated, shrugged their shoulders, saying they would not be responsible for his life if he disregarded their orders. They drove him from one watering-place to another, put him through cures and cures and after-cures which necessitated his foregoing all the delicacies of the table, to which the uninterrupted habit of more than thirty years had accustomed him. Until now the small number of people who adhered to

202

the rules of the cure in a watering-place had always been a subject for scorn with him. He argued that they over-ate themselves all the year round, and then fancied that a month's abstinence would cure their maladies, — a fallacy which was ridiculous, even dangerous, for the body demanded fair treatment, and would not allow liberties of this kind to be taken with it.

With these views, it was not surprising that whenever he felt indisposed, he attributed the cause to his having nourished himself insufficiently, or to the food having been indifferently prepared. Knowing this feature in his philosophy, a very clever doctor sent him to a place in the Swiss mountains where you could not get much to eat because it was not there. He had to content himself with bathing in countless waters, putting himself under the care of the masseur, the pedicure, the manicure, and cursing at his servant. But it was terribly dull, — a dog's life, as he called it, — and he grumbled all the time, and was known at the little Waldhaus where he stayed as a very ill-tempered man. Once when an old lady burst into ecstasy over the colour of the mountains which could be seen from the dinner-table, and which, towards evening, were suffused with a rose-coloured glow from the setting sun, the Prince grew quite angry. " The mountains! the mountains! " he growled, as the old lady grew more and more enthusiastic, " yes, but you cannot eat the mountains!" and he pushed away his plate of sausage, and threw his fork upon it with an air of intense disgust.

The strictness of the diet was killing him. It made life impossible; and, finally, feeling that anything was preferable to the discomfort of a bad cuisine, he determined, in the early part of September, to go to the Lake of Como. For nearly two months he had obeyed the doctors. He argued that he was not strong enough to endure it any longer; the doctors would succeed in ruining the finest constitution in the world.

Cecilia

For a few days he flitted about the lake; and, on deciding that the cooking was best at Tremezzina, he ordered his servant to transfer all his luggage to the hotel, and prepared himself for a prolonged stay. The place was full of people during September and the early part of October, and he spent his time very agreeably, adapting himself with the ease of the club-man without family ties to the " organised egoism " of the hotel, where people lived their lives in odd, disjointed fragments, passing close to one another, even touching one another, in a cold, unproductive intimacy.

He was extremely popular among the inmates, in each of whom he found something to amuse him; and he was voted charming by the ladies, of whose society he was very fond, and to whom he made himself infinitely agreeable. He would gather them round him in a circle, and tell amusing stories about himself, based upon a few facts which he moulded and embellished with a rich fancy until they represented him as the central figure in an impossible romance. The ladies were interested and puzzled, because he never paid them any individual court, but contrived to make them sigh for his company in a body. Had he made love to them, he would have appeared ridiculous; but his love-making was always done in private, and was confined to a disreputable world who lived on him and laughed at him, secure in the certainty that no laughter could ever penetrate through his vanity, which was as impervious as a suit of armour. So complete was it, so untouched (for his wealth had spared him the outrages which the necessity of making money inflicts), that it made him a king in the world which he created for himself.

Moreover, he won himself many friends by an unbridled generosity, in the exercise of which he enjoyed a sound moral sentiment to which his vanity largely contributed; for whenever he gave — and he gave freely — he felt as if he had satisfied a moral need; in fact, of the luxuries in which he indulged, generosity was perhaps the only one which took the form of a virtue, and consequently he enjoyed a peculiar exaltation from the satisfaction of his desire to give, to which less unscrupulous persons could never hope to attain. And when he had given away a sum of money, or made a present, he would be weak enough to fancy for a moment that he was not so irreligious as he was in the habit of believing himself; he fell into the state of that great portion of the world which calls itself religious, and vaguely identifies the deity of its religion with the less contemptible actions in its own life.

Amongst other occasions, he certainly felt that he was acting as an agent of the deity when he lent Dornstein money at Emilienbad; for he knew that he would never get it back, but possibly Dornstein might secretly offer up a prayer of thanks for deliverance to *his* deity;

and Pezarin felt an inward glow of satisfaction
at the thought.

He spent his time in the hotel, dining, sleeping, and dressing himself, or rather being
dressed, for his servant waited on him, hand
and foot, and the only trouble to which he put
himself was that of selecting what clothes he
would wear, a task onerous enough, as his
wardrobe was very large, and every article of
apparel, from his collar and tie down to his
socks, demanded a careful consideration.

When he had any spare time, he read English and French novels; and though he never
opened a page of any other branch in literature,
he expressed a great contempt for fiction. For
him there were only two classes of novel: that
which was faithful to life, and which he declared
to have no attraction for him, because when
you knew life you did n't want a book about
it; and that which was false to life, wildly
impossible, and which was all very well for
young men, but of no interest to a man of

sense. Youth and sense were always terms that excluded each other in his philosophy.

Towards the end of October the hotel emptied rapidly. At last an old Italian General was the only one person besides himself who remained in it, the rest of the people changing from day to day, and growing fewer and fewer. The old General had stayed in Tremezzina during the whole of the summer, — a fact which always excited surprise among visitors to the hotel, for the Lakes were well known to be stifling during the months of July and August. But the old man never understood their surprise, and murmured, " I like to be warm ! I like to be warm !" He was very infirm, and his face was very shrivelled. In the evening when people sat bare-headed on the terrace by the lake, eager to breathe a cooler air after the heat of the day, the old General rarely ventured out, and when he did, he always wrapped himself round with a thick shawl which provoked the laughter of the others; but the old man gathered the folds closer about him, murmured, " One catches cold so easily," and shuffled away disconsolately.

Pezarin laughed at him with the other inmates of the hotel; but though he found him an agreeable topic of conversation, he was not at all inclined to be left alone with him in the hotel, and he began to think of leaving.

One evening not more than six people took their places at the table d'hôte : three men besides the Prince and the General and a young and pretty lady with a little girl whom she fed during most of the dinner-time, and for whom the General displayed that interest and kindliness which only very old people show to those who are very young, while the face of the mother showed plainly a keen pleasure in the attention that her child excited.

As soon as dinner was over, the lady and the little girl went upstairs into their apartments, the General retired to the reading-

room to glance at "Il Papagallo," and the
three men strolled on to the terrace, where
they seated themselves at the edge of the
lake.

The night was warm and cloudless, and on
the glassy surface of the water rested the
faint images of stars reflected from the sky.
The trees in the gardens that fronted the lake
did not stir, a stillness held the air prisoner.

The two elder men began to smoke and
talk, while the third, a young man — the son
of one of the others — watched the swarm of
moths and other insects which circled round
and round a gas-lamp rising from the stone
parapet close to which they were sitting.

From his seat further down the terrace
Prince Pezarin could hear the voices of the
speakers, and he soon gathered from their
conversation that they were commercial travellers. The young man's father was entirely
absorbed in conversation with his companion :
they were comparing their experiences in busi-

ness, and with the astuteness of men whose lives were spent in the difficult pursuit of making money, were each, under the pretence of keeping the other company, endeavouring to extract from him some piece of information useful to himself.

Meanwhile the young man sat in silence, drinking for the first time in his life the full glory of an Italian night. Lines of poems that he had learned at school, and at the university, rose to his memory, as he gazed with longing eyes at the lake. He thought how sweet it would be to lie on his back in a boat and drift along, his eyes fixed on the harvest of stars with which the heaven above him was sown. Opposite were dark masses of hills and the twinkling yellow lights of another village which crept down to the edge of the water. And the air was full of the perfume of flowers and the strong smell of the earth, which was giving out in vapour the heat poured into it by the sun during all the day. Round him he could feel the presence of luxuriant foliage, which, in the intoxication of his delight, he longed to embrace; just as in fancy he longed to pluck a star from the sky above him. . . .

And a stone's throw from him, supremely unconscious of the beauty of the night and the magic tranquillity of the scene, his mind travelling serenely in the realms of commerce, sat his father, calmly dilating on the peculiarities which distinguished the great firm of " Weber, Weber & Weber," from that of any other house in the city of London.

Meanwhile the Prince smoked on in silence, wrapped in that perfect physical content which had been created in him by an excellent dinner and an old bottle of wine, to the after-effects of which he regarded the natural beauty of the scene as an appropriate background. Occasionally the smell of the merchant's cigar mingled with that of his own, and he reflected that, if he were not very much mistaken, the other must be smoking a Cabinet Corona y Corona.

Glancing along the terrace, he had observed that the seat of the young man was vacant, and soon the conversation of the two gentlemen reached him only in fragments, broken by the sound of fioriture passages on the piano, which floated through the open window of the drawing-room to where he sat. The incongruousness of the words and the music tickled him.

In a corner of the drawing-room in which the young man was playing, and which was quite dark, sat the figure of an old man who did not move a muscle for fear that his presence should be observed. He was wrapped in a shawl, for the night air which came in through the open window chilled him.

But the music stirred him so deeply that he trembled every now and then with emotion, and tears began to well from his feeble eyes. His mind was in the past, wandering through passages of his life,—that life which was to end soon, alone, alone, without wife or friend or child to help him! Why?—God knows. He had not been different to other men, but it had happened so; and the music filled him with the longing as of a little child that cries for the broken toys strewn round it to be whole again; and it touched him so that he wept. . . .

And in the same room sat the young man, entirely absorbed in the egoism of his pursuit translating into sound the intensity of his feeling for the stars and the lake and the mysterious beauty of the night; and the old Italian stole away unperceived.

When the young man had exhausted himself at the piano, he strolled down to the lake and seated himself on the stone parapet, close to where the Prince was seated, still smoking.

Cecilia

"Ah! voilà mon affaire," said Pezarin to himself. He wanted to find out the name of the brand of cigars which the merchant was smoking, and he did not want to disturb himself, for he had settled into a comfortable attitude in his seat, and four fingers of his right hand nestled in the cross pocket of his mess jacket.

"A very fine night," he said, by way of opening the conversation. But the young man continued to gaze at the lake without answering; the reflection of the lights of the opposite village in the water seemed to his fancy like feathers of gold, and the images of the stars like waterlilies.

"I see you are a poet," said the Prince, after a few minutes. "Do you smoke?" he added, with a brusque access of politeness, as he drew from his pocket a silver cigarette-case, which he handed to the young man, who turned towards him, while a faint smile, born of his fancy, lingered on his face. He shook his head.

Cecilia

"Ah, you do not smoke!" said Pezarin, closing the case with a click, and replacing it in his pocket, from the corner of which his thumb strayed carelessly. "You lose one of the great pleasures of life. Poems are all very well — J'en ai fais moi-même; but that was when I was young and worshipped your Byron. Now I worship cigars. For instance, a cigar like that which your father has been smoking, that is worth ten volumes of poetry to me." (It might be an Amontillado of the '78 crop, he reflected to himself.)

A dragon-fly flashed in the air, which the fancy of the boy turned to the form of a tiny winged horse.

"Peugh!" ejaculated the Prince, as it brushed the tip of his nose with its wings, "that's the worst of the open air, the insects are a perfect nuisance."

The young man was trying to imagine himself in thirty years' time, and wondering whether he would think like the man in front of him, and would become a cynic too, whether a veil would creep over his eyes and blind him to the beauty of nature; and the Prince puffed lazily at his cigar, silenced by the unsociability of his companion, and reflecting that he too was like this boy in the past, ever so long ago, before he had fallen in love with the German actress in Aix-les-Bains.

That was the time when he had raved about Lord Byron, and spent hours and hours dreaming over "The Corsair" and "Lara" and "Childe Harold." His mind wandered then through forests of tall trees through which the wind whispered, forests wherein flowed countless streams that shone golden in the sun, silver beneath the moon, a vague country of the imagination, into which the living figure of neither man nor woman insinuated itself. That was the time when nature, his sole possession, was beautiful to him as the form of a woman whom he had neither seen nor touched, but only dreamed.

Cecilia

As he mused, the boy turned away to the lake again; and now from the distance came the sound of singing on the water, and a boat decorated with lanterns, and full of men and women, swam into sight, the voices growing stronger and stronger, and then fainter and fainter.

And to the boy, the boat was a marvellous vision peopled with gods and goddesses, mystic, wonderful; and the eyes of the Prince laughed as, in the sounds that were borne over the water to him, he recognised the words of a ribald song.

"Edward," cried a harsh, querulous voice farther down the terrace, "Edward, where are you?"

The boy rose from his seat as if to go.

The Prince threw the end of his cigar into the lake, and it hissed faintly as it met the water.

"Don't stay for me," he said sarcastically, "I can do without your poetical conversation. Go along. And while your father is earning the money to bring you here, go and write a sonnet to the moon which no one but yourself will ever want to read! Go along. What are you waiting for? But stop a minute. I am curious, and want to know your name.

" Well, Mr. Edward Mason," resumed the Prince, when the boy had satisfied his curiosity, " perhaps you will take longer to learn your lesson than the majority. There are people who wake up late in life. Poor people! But one day when you are sitting on this seat and smoking a fine Corona cigar (it must be Corona after all), you will laugh at yourself as I laugh at you. Pardon! Good-night!"

He held his hand out and the young man shook it and walked away, and the Prince leaned back in his seat. The time when nature was his sole possession, and beautiful as a woman he had never seen, was gone. Therese Melany headed the list of living

Cecilia

women who had come to disillusionise the day-dreams of a boy over a book of poems. She had been the first to stand between the young Prince and the book whose pages she had darkened so that he could not see the lines any more.

And as he sat looking into the clear, brilliant night, his eyes fixed in a glazed stare, he could only remember one line out of the days when nature had come first in his thoughts, and the undefined, vague, unreal woman had served as a simile. And in that line the poet called a storm at night lovely in its strength as was the light of a dark eye in woman.

And another line jostled this one in his memory, one he had written himself when his passion for the Melany was at its height; and in this line nature was used to serve the pur-pose of the simile, and the real woman came first :

"Theresa !
Your smile is like the sunrise on the mountains ! "

Cecilia

And as time had gone on, the Prince reflected with a smile that he had dispensed with the simile altogether; and at this point in his meditations he rose and went indoors. And as he glanced carelessly at the Visitors' Book, which lay open in the marble hall under a solitary jet of gas, he saw by the freshness of the ink that there had been a new arrival, and looking closer at the page he read in a small, undecided handwriting:

ALBERT STERN, BARRISTER, LONDON.

And underneath in a large, bold hand:

CECILIA STERN.

Pezarin began at once to think of the Cecilia of Emilienbad, and to wonder if this could be the same. He looked towards the bureau to see if any one were still up of whom he could make inquiries. But everywhere it was dark; the old General had gone to bed long ago; the lady and her child were both at rest in their room; not a servant could either be seen or heard. The Prince made his way across the deserted hall, mounted the staircase, which echoed under his footsteps, and consoled himself with the reflection that in all probability he would see the newcomers on the morrow.

He went to bed and fell asleep almost immediately, while in the room next to him on one side lay Edward Mason, his window open and his blinds not yet drawn. The boy had flung himself upon the bed to gaze up at the multitude of stars with which the sky was peopled, and, as he dreamed with eyes wide open, the poetry of his youth clothed each of them with the semblance of a flower wherein lay hidden the secrets of life.

And two doors away from him, separated only from him by the Prince, who was snoring now at regular intervals, lay Cecilia, the girl on whom had fallen years ago the cloak of that imagination with which on this night he was wrapping round the stars.

A perfect stillness now fell over that little

Cecilia

world, gathered together in the vast hotel : and
those stars shone peacefully down upon the
cynic, plunged in the oblivion of brute sleep,
upon the poet, tossing feverishly from side to
side, upon the man and woman newly wedded,
upon the mother, over whose face a divine
smile was passing as she dreamed of the child
asleep by her side, and upon the old man in
whose feeble body the last spark of life was
swiftly growing cold.

II

WHEN Pezarin opened his shutters the next morning at ten o'clock, the sun was so strong that it made him blink his eyes.

A porter was wheeling across the paved court-yard a truck of clean-looking luggage marked with a large S in white paint. In front of the hotel portico stood an open carriage, and the Prince watched for some time in the hope of seeing the departure of the people for whom the carriage waited, but for some time no one came. The horses flapped their ears backwards and forwards to keep off the cloud of flies that swarmed round them. Now and then one of them curled up a hind leg and stamped on the paved court, which rang with the sound of the hoof. A fat coachman, in soiled livery of blue and gold, sat on the box, holding the reins loosely in his hands, while his head, covered with a broad tall hat made of shining material and adorned with a gold band, sank lower and lower on his chest, as the sun beat mercilessly upon him.

The Prince was just growing tired of watching, and was about to ring for his servant to shave him, when a young lady and gentleman stepped into the carriage. The young lady at once opened a white silk sunshade, which she held over her head, but not before Pezarin had recognised her.

"It is Mademoiselle Rayner," he said to himself, "married, I suppose, to that man with the yellow skin who stoops so much. Grand Dieu : il n'est pas beau celui-là — et juif au bout — du nez." He had not much time to scrutinise the pair, for the carriage soon drove off, while the Prince, with an unopened razor-case in his hand, stood smiling at his own witticism.

When, after performing an elaborate toilette, he came downstairs, he found that the

Masons and the commercial traveller had also left the hotel; they had taken the early steamer to Como, in which town Mr. Mason had business to transact. "It begins to be triste here," thought Pezarin to himself as he pictured in his mind the table d'hôte dinner tête-à-tête with the old Italian General. Perhaps the young lady and the child might add their presence, but even then —

As his servant was putting him to bed that night, he told him to begin packing up, for he had determined to leave in a few days. He spent two months of the winter in Rome, three in Vienna, and then went to Paris for the spring season, much fortified, and prepared to renew all the exertions which were involved in the business of pleasure.

Meanwhile, at least two people in London had found the winter very dull.

Mrs. Rayner felt her isolation keenly. While the Sterns were in London, the absence of her daughter affected her less closely; but towards the end of October they returned to the Riviera, and Mrs. Rayner was left alone in Davenport Lodge.

She used to sit in the study every afternoon, and try to think of the names of people who possibly might come in to tea. But as one day succeeded another without anybody calling, she began to realise that now that her daughter was no longer at home, the circle of her friends would be considerably narrowed. She was compelled to console herself with the hope of an abundance of news from Cecilia, which never came. The girl's letters to her mother were always very short and written in a hurry, just as she was leaving one place for another: and to her mother's repeated question as to when they might be expected home, she made no reply. At first Mrs. Rayner used to go down three or four times a week to the house in Berkeley Square, which was in the hands of the builders and decorators. She gave directions to the men, cancelled them, asked innumerable questions, and finally had a sharp altercation with the foreman, who said he had received his instructions from Mr. Stern, and could not carry out the work satisfactorily if he were constantly being interrupted.

Deprived of this pastime, Mrs. Rayner took refuge in the company of Miss Savory, to an account of whose rheumatic sufferings she listened patiently, in consideration of the amiability with which the old lady sympathised with an unhappy mother's grievances. The two ladies had not been so much together since their school days, to which Miss Savory had the tact never to allude.

Herminia was glad of the companionship of her friend, for her rheumatism had troubled her so much during the winter that in the care of her body her love of society and gossip had subsided for a time. "She did not feel well enough to exert herself in the entertainment of visitors, and was grateful to Mrs. Rayner whenever she called at her flat. During their conversations she never failed to introduce the subject of the Colonel, for whom Mrs. Rayner's respect had increased ever since he had been the means of disposing of her old silver to advantage.

When one morning towards the close of February Miss Savory received from Mrs. Rayner a letter containing the news that Cecilia would be home in a month's time, the announcement disconcerted her considerably; for she knew that she would see a great deal less of her friend as soon as her daughter was within reach. She was a little comforted by the prospect of the warm weather which was soon coming, and, as if to confirm her hopes, while she was reading the letter at her breakfast-table a ray of sun darted through the mild blue sky and fell slanting through the window upon her mantel-piece. Miss Savory was quite thrilled by the circumstance, and gazed absently at the mass of photographs and china ornaments with which the shelf was crowded. Then she noticed how very dusty everything looked. But soon her attention was fixed upon a sprig of orange blossom which appeared above the neck of a tiny vase. The sun fell pitilessly upon the faded bloom and the yellow shrivelled leaves, and Miss Savory began to reflect. How withered it looked! — and yet it could not be long ago; and then she sighed as she reckoned that nine months had passed since Cecilia's wedding.

"What shall I do without the company of my dear Emma?" she wrote to Mrs. Rayner, "for of course, now that your daughter is coming, you will have heaps to do. But, instead of your coming to me, when my leg permits I must come to you. I shall be at home every Wednesday as soon as the warm weather has set in, and if I am only well enough, I shall enjoy seeing all my friends."

Miss Savory's flat was in West Kensington, and the building of which it formed the first floor, a tall, narrow jumble of red brick and iron-work of a very aggressive character, was called Veronica Mansions; soon after she had written to Mrs. Rayner, she began to be at home on Wednesdays. On these occasions she always stayed indoors in the morning " to arrange," this being one of the joys of her life. The night before, she would imagine to herself how the room would look if the furniture were disposed in a new order. She would put the tables and chairs through a series of permutations and combinations in her mind; and she usually spent a restless night planning a new scheme for the morrow. By the time she reached the second Wednesday in May, her invention grew to be sorely taxed, for, though the number of ways of arranging the room were almost infinite, a large number of them had to be discarded as being inartistic, and an almost equally large number were impracticable. Consequently, Miss Savory was much agitated on the night before the second Wednesday in May. Her brain refused to work rationally. All kinds of absurd suggestions rushed into her mind, such as putting the piano in the middle of the room and serving tea on it, or placing it up against the fireplace to hide the grate. For a long time she could not sleep, and then, when she fell at last into a restless slumber, she dreamed that her drawing-room was full of people, but that there were no chairs for them to sit upon; so she ran about looking for chairs, which, in accordance with the rules of nightmares, were nowhere to be found.

The next morning as soon as breakfast was over, she set to work as usual. She always had the servant to help her, as some of the furniture was too heavy for her to move alone, although for a woman of nearly sixty she was remarkably active. In the midst of the turmoil and confusion that she soon contrived to create, she would suddenly stand still, and, surveying the room with a critical eye, she would say, " Have we had that before, Susan ? " to which the servant, who vainly tried to remember the number of different arrangements that had already been executed on former Wednesdays, would reply in a perplexed tone of voice, " I don't *think* so, m'm."

As a rule, Miss Savory had only time to get into her purple velvet dress when the first visitor rang the bell. She would then hasten into the room and take up her position, which had also been carefully worked out during the labours of the morning, so that when the visitor was announced, she looked as if she had been in the room for hours, reading, and she would remove her spectacles and advance to meet her guest with the air of a person who has just been interrupted in the midst of a most absorbing occupation.

A very pretty touch in the arrangement of the room was the careless distribution of some loose sheets of music on the top of a cottage piano, at one end of which a violin was placed at a becoming angle. The case and the bow were stowed away behind the instrument, which cut across a corner of the room. The keyboard was always kept open. This effect was repeated on several occasions: it formed the predominant note in the scheme, the climax in the pictorial drama to which the disposition of the furniture was designed to lead. The eye travelled round the walls, covered with a confusion of looking-glasses, pictures, photographs, china ornaments on brackets, Japanese fans, crept in and out of tables, chairs, and painted milking-stools, and finally alighted on this piano, which was surmounted by a large engraving of the Queen, as a supreme piece of decoration.

Occasionally, Miss Savory would be asked if the violin was hers, to which she replied, " No ; it belongs to the Colonel ; he comes of an evening sometimes, and we play together a little. Have you seen the shawl he brought

with him from India? It is very handsome;"
and she would go to a cabinet, unlock it, and
take from it a shawl of many bright colours,
very neatly folded, which she handed round
for the inspection of her visitors.

On the afternoon of this second Wednesday
in May, Miss Savory had quite a crowd of
visitors. In fact, she made a mental note that
her newest arrangement, though it was everything that the eye could desire, was dangerous;
because, in order to secure a particular effect,
she had put one chair behind the piano, thus
losing a seat, and, if another person had come
in, her distressing dream of the night before
might, to some extent, have proved a pro-
phecy, it being impossible to extricate the
chair from the back of the piano without
considerable difficulty, and every other seat
in the room being already occupied. However, as it was, nothing of so serious a nature
occurred.

At a quarter to six, the dashing little Mrs.

Sherbetter, who was at present being piloted into " smart society " by Lady Killigrew, stood at the door with her head slightly on one side.

" May I come in ? " she said. " It's so late, that I was almost afraid to come. But I have been driving in the park."

She was very prettily dressed, and looked as if she had only just stepped out of her room. Miss Savory was charmed that she had come.

" Come and sit by me," she said. " How did the park look ? "

" Lovely," replied Mrs. Sherbetter. " So full. The Princess of Wales was there — which, you know, always makes the park full. Mrs. Stanton was driving the loveliest pair of greys I ever saw — and oh, I had almost forgotten — whom do you think I saw ? You'll never guess, so I'd better tell you at once. Cecilia Rayner, Mrs. — Mrs. — what is her name ? "

" Stern," said Miss Savory.

" Stern," repeated Mrs. Sherbetter, " that is

the name," and then she relapsed into silence, while the attention of the whole circle of ladies was earnestly fixed upon her.

"How did she look?" said a lady at last, when it became obvious that Mrs. Sherbetter was not going to deliver herself of further information until it was solicited.

"Why, my dear, you never saw such a sight in your life! She's completely gone off. I never saw such a change. And you know how beautifully she used to dress; well, I never saw such a muddle as she wore. It was all rags and tatters of different colours, and she wore a hat so large that her face looked small and pinched beneath it — almost ugly. I was astonished. I scarcely recognised her."

"Was her husband with her?" asked Miss Savory, whose friendship with the Rayners never stood in her way when they were being discussed.

"Yes," answered Mrs. Sherbetter. "He

was sitting by her side with his head buried in his shoulders. He looked the picture of misery. I never did think him a handsome man, but he looked quite broken," and she hunched up her shoulders, making her thin black satin cape wrinkle, in her imitation of Albert Stern. "She was talking very hard at him as we flashed past," she added. "She had not time to bow to us, even if she saw us, which was not likely, as she seemed absorbed in telling her husband something. What it was I don't know."

"And what was the carriage like?"

"Oh, a handsome victoria, with a good pair of bay horses; not as handsome as Mrs. Stanton's, but still quite good enough."

"I never thought Cecilia Rayner so handsome as everybody else did," said a lady, a little tentatively.

Mrs. Sherbetter at once defended Cecilia, whom she allowed no one to criticise adversely but herself.

"Oh, she was a beautiful girl! No one could deny that. Not every one's style, perhaps, but a beautiful girl for all that can be said. But you should see her now. I assure you, her face quite shocked me — I turned quite pale when we had passed. It made me quite sad."

As Mrs. Sherbetter began to grow a little sentimental, there was an appropriate silence for about a minute, which was broken by a lady asking:

"How long have they been married?"

"About a year," said Miss Savory. "Don't you remember," she went on, turning to Mrs. Sherbetter, "they were married in the summer. It was just such another fine day as this. I brought away a piece of the orange blossom, and kept it ever since; it is on my mantel-piece now," and she pointed to the discoloured little spray in the small vase. "She certainly looked handsome then."

"I never saw a more beautiful bride," said

Mrs. Sherbetter, and then she went on to talk of Mrs. Rayner and the vicar and Davenport Lodge, until the silvery bell of Miss Savory's clock struck six, and the ladies took their leave.

III

To Montagu Stern, Esq.

27 Duke Street, London, W.

PARIS, 25th March, 1887.

DEAR MONTY, — In a week we shall be home.
We have been in Italy, Switzerland, and France; but
somehow I don't seem to remember much of the places
we have seen. I cannot yet understand how lucky I
am, although I think every day convinces me of it
more and more. Cecilia laughs at me, and calls me
"baby," a name which I suppose I deserve. We get
on famously, and if all married life is as easy as the last
few months have been, I don't see why people make
such a fuss about it, and talk of it as a lottery and all
that. Why, it is as straight-forward as possible! We
never disagree, because we both want the same things;
and if Cecilia wants something which I don't think I
want, I find that I am mistaken and that I do want it,
because most of all I am anxious to want what she
wants. There you have the secret in a nut-shell.

"And this is the man who was never going to
marry," I can hear you mumble as you glance over

the page. Well, a change of view is a sign of progress and I am not ashamed to own it.

"Perhaps you will change again: the honeymoon is no criterion," you say.

Nonsense, my dear fellow. A man must be crazy who could not get on with Cecilia. She is as gentle and amiable as — well, I can't find the word, so never mind. Besides, who could not put up with a great deal from any one who is so beautiful? And she is beautiful — adorable! People turn round in the streets to look at her. When I tell her that this constant admiration will turn her head, she laughs and says, "I am accustomed to it. It has n't turned my head yet: it has n't influenced my choice of a husband. Why should it influence me now? I don't care 'that' for it!" and then she snaps her fingers and laughs as only she can laugh. Goodness, how I rave, but to you I don't mind. Only remember that this is a private letter. I believe if I had n't gone ahead pretty boldly, you would have stolen the ground from under my feet yourself, you rascal. But what a long time ago it seems already, since we sat under the Ercole in dear old Cannes.

Of course we have made a great many plans for the future. I shall go on reading in Chambers, because a man must have an occupation, you know, and it will please the old man. Perhaps in time I may get a mild practice; although, of course, I don't care a straw for the profession, and thank the Lord we are rich enough, in the long run, to be lazy.

C. and I went to the Opéra Comique last night, and heard a lovely thing. We can't get one of the tunes out of our heads, and have been singing all the morning: "Zon, ra, ra, Zon, ra, ra." What a voice she has, and what exquisite French she can talk! I suppose the house will be ready for us by our return. If not, we can go to a hotel for a few days. One more or less won't matter after our wanderings.

Your affectionate brother,

ALBERT STERN.

A week later, the young couple arrived in London, and were met at the station by Montagu and Mrs. Rayner, both of whom accompanied them to their house in Berkeley Square, where they all dined together. Cecilia was delighted with everything; and Mrs. Rayner took every exclamation of approval as a compliment to herself, for she declared that she had spared herself no trouble to bring every-thing into perfect order, and expressed her satisfaction that in spite of the workmen, who were always troublesome, she had succeeded in getting everything ready in time to receive the travellers.

For a time Cecilia busied herself with her house, enjoying to the full the sense of personal possession which it conferred on her. Her long absence from her mother, and the freedom from her control which her position afforded, contrib-uted to establish a more amicable understand-ing than had hitherto reigned between them.

Albert allowed his wife to have her own way. Only occasionally he murmured at some new extravagance in which she wished to in-dulge; but usually she was so submissive and considerate to him that the incident ended in his repenting his economy, and buying for her something twice as costly as that for which she had asked him in the first instance. She had an infinite tact in accepting these gifts, mingling her surprise with a flood of gratitude that recompensed him a thousandfold for the sacrifice he had made, for he was not entirely free to spend as much as he liked. His father allowed him a handsome sum of money a year, but he had not yet transferred the capital to his son, considering that, at all events for a time, it was wise that the young man should realise that he was under an obligation for the money he received. David Stern was not mean; but, like all men who have earned large fortunes by their own ingenuity or exertions, he enjoyed the power which accompanies wealth, and was loath to part with any portion of that power. Albert was consequently anxious, within the early years of his married life, to curb his expenditure within certain limits.

He went down every morning to Chambers in the Temple, and idled away his time until the evening. While the successful lawyer with whom he " read " was dictating pleadings, in a loud, rasping voice, to the clerk who took them down on blue foolscap, in a large, straggling schoolboy hand, Albert sat at a desk heaped up with text-books and law reports, and gazed out of the window upon the river.

" Go on, go on," the eminent lawyer would say to the clerk, in an irritated voice. " Why the devil can't you write quicker? ' Paragraph 7. On the blank month of blank year the defendant company entered into an agreement with the plaintiff whereby in consideration of payment by the plaintiff of the sum of blank pounds the said defendant company would execute repairs as enumerated on pages five, six, and seven of the exhibit marked X 35 by the blank day of blank blank.' Have you got that down? Oh, dear, oh, dear ! Why can't you go a little quicker ? "

Meanwhile, Albert watched the cabs in miniature flying along the embankment, and the more mysterious barges floating along the river, swimming into a shower of crimson and purple sparks which trembled and died away on the surface of the water as the summer clouds swept over the sun.

And while the light was playing golden pranks upon the river, and the lawyer was rolling out his verbose sentences to the clerk, over Cecilia a great change was passing. Her temper grew more uneven. Sometimes she sought to quarrel with her husband for no ostensible reason. At other times, she was all gentleness and repentance. Once he remonstrated against the extravagant appearance of a dress which she had bought, and she upbraided him as if he had done her an injury. She used occasionally to drive down to the Temple and fetch him away for a visit to the park. But soon she made excuses, said it tired her too much, and made up reasons to account for her behaviour, which only mystified him all the more.

At the end of June, when he knew that she

pregnant

was enceinte, he would have liked to kiss her, and drew her towards him; but she turned aside irritably.

"Not now," she said. "Wait."

He was distressed. He wanted her to rejoice with him already; but she was resolute, and grew so unreasonable that at last he was forced to promise her not to talk any more about it for a time. When he looked perplexed, she smiled, stroked his face and said:

"You don't understand women, Albert;" and he was satisfied, persuading himself that his marriage with Cecilia was to teach him the great lessons of life which had hitherto been unknown to him.

They went into the country in August, at the doctor's command; but Cecilia grew so ill that, at the beginning of September, they were compelled to return to town, where they could have the best medical attendance. Here she rapidly grew worse; and soon it was judged advisable for Mrs. Rayner to take up her quarters in Berkeley Square. Physicians were called in, and a nurse was engaged. Albert was distracted, not knowing what to expect next. He sat alone in his room crying, for hours, and no one dared to give him any hope. When he went into the sick room, Cecilia abused him, and made fun of him before the nurse. Once he tried to put her pillows straight for her, and she struck him in the face. At last the doctors forbade him to enter the room. And for three weeks he did not see her, but hung about outside her door, on the landings, on the stairs, intercepting the servants, the doctors, the nurses, terrified by the sight of medical appliances, and sickened by the perfumes that came from the room where she lay. Sometimes he sat nearly all day looking out of the dining-room window upon the square, trying to interest himself in the carriages that passed, and rushing to the front door himself whenever he saw the servant of any of his friends stop at the house to make inquiries, so that no noise might be made, even by the ringing of a bell. He refused to see visitors, and before long ordered a bulletin to be posted outside the door. When he recognised people who were standing to read it, he hid himself carefully behind the curtain so that he could not be seen. His own people were abroad, travelling, and, though they were the only persons who could have given him any comfort, he was determined not to send for them. By isolating himself, he was aggravating his grief; but he was making it more his own, which gave him a kind of queer, savage satisfaction. He began to talk to himself again, a habit which had forsaken him since his marriage, but which now came upon him again with renewed force. He could not forget the horror in her face when Cecilia had struck him while he was trying to arrange her pillows. The pain of that moment was infinite; and over and over again the scene shaped itself before his unwilling eyes, so that he was driven to blame himself, in order to excuse the woman he loved. "She did n't know, she did n't know," he kept murmuring to himself; "she was delirious: the doctors said so. It was my own fault for bothering her," and he tried to strengthen his belief in her innocence, when her mother was told also that it would be better for her not to enter the sick room. Mrs. Rayner talked very little: all her emotions were expressed in her movements. She was grave, mysterious, wore a look of self-contained meditation, and frequently rose from the table at which she ate her meals with her son-in-law, and left the room, without assigning any reason for acting in this way. A sort of tacit enmity seemed to spring up between the two, as if the affection of each for Cecilia were an insult to the other. Mrs. Rayner assumed the airs of the protecting mother, which implied a certain contempt for the abject devotion of the husband *without whom all the mischief would not have happened.*

Cecilia

For seven weeks, Cecilia lay between life and death, and the household were in a constant state of alarm. Albert used to wake in the night and listen, until he was almost mad with fear. He could hear Cecilia groaning, the nurses whispering, the sound of doors stealthily opened and closed again. Creeping out upon the landing, where a single jet of gas burned low, he would look down upon the floor below, where Cecilia lay. The house became a perpetual nightmare to him. All the expensive ornaments and furniture with which it was filled, and which were once a source of fresh pleasure each time that he looked upon them, became oppressive and hideous; they seemed to emphasise the misfortune which had fallen upon him, to add an irony to the pain of the situation.

When the child was born, triumph shone from the eyes of Mrs. Rayner; but the doctors still shook their heads when Albert inquired of the condition of the mother. She was so

terribly weak, that though there was a possibility of her recovering with the greatest
care, they could not conscientiously say that
she was yet out of danger. The slightest
accident might be fatal. However, up till
now she had agreeably disappointed their
gravest fears, and there was some hope for
the future. The child, a boy, was exceedingly
delicate, but with care should give no cause for
excessive alarm. The doctor fancied he detected
a tinge of disappointment in the mother's face
when she heard that her child was a son; but he
did not communicate his impression either to
Albert or Mrs. Rayner, both of whom, for different reasons, were quite satisfied on this score.

To Albert, exhausted with despair and
physical fatigue, the birth of a son occasioned
a feeling of peculiar exaltation; it was an omen
of future happiness; and one day, when Mrs.
Rayner entered the drawing-room unnoticed,
she saw him standing opposite a looking-glass
and smiling at the reflection of his face.

IV

THERE were times during her illness when
Cecilia felt so weak that it almost seemed to
her as if her body had perished, and that
only a still, clear consciousness remained. At
such moments the people round her would
seem infinitely far off and unreal, and the
figures of her mother and of her husband
floated through her mind like puppets of a
few inches high. All the circumstances in
which she was placed, she realised with a clear-
ness of reason which she had never possessed
before: she was on the point of death; they
were all very kind to her, and she was infinitely grateful; she would die without a murmur; only she had something to explain.
She suffered an intense longing to make an
honest declaration to some one who would
understand, so that her whole life might not

be a lie. At least at the end she would stand clear with the world. Her confession would be so easy to understand, something like this: I did not love the man whom they gave me for a husband. I could not; it was not my fault; and I said yes, because it was so hard to go on in the old way. That is all.

And while the thought conveyed by these words floated vaguely in her head, she was too weak to speak. She would turn her head on the pillow and gaze with such pain-stricken eyes, that the nurse would come and put fresh rags on her burning forehead. But even if she could have spoken, who would have listened? The nurse would not understand; besides, she felt that only one person was fit to hear her, and that person was a phantom created by the need she felt to speak, — some sweet woman, older than herself, who would smile fondly at her, press her hand, and say, " I understand." If that wish could have been granted to her, she felt that she could have even begun to love

her husband with a love founded on the
generosity of his forgiveness, when he knew
the whole truth.   She would have looked
once into his face, to see that the blow had
not extinguished the light of love from his
eyes, and then she would have closed her
eyes in peace never to open them again.   But
the saviour was nowhere at hand, and the
agony of her isolation was terrible.   It quick-
ened the spark of vitality that yet burned in
her enfeebled frame; it formed the turning
point in her illness.   The death that she coveted was not to be granted to her; she longed
for no other; so she strove to live, and the
body triumphed over the spirit.

As she grew stronger, the recollection of
such moments faded from her mind.   The
regeneration of her body was a source of physical relief, a greater luxury than she had ever
yet experienced.   She abandoned herself to
it wholly, without restraint.   She indulged
to the full the purely selfish instincts of the

sick person, demanded to be satisfied in every caprice, and summoned the doctor on endless occasions when his presence was unnecessary. She would keep him talking as long as possible, and always made an elaborate toilette before he arrived, making the nurse dress her hair in little waves over her forehead, and put a silk quilt embroidered with roses on the bed. She insisted on Albert going out, and, when he remonstrated with her, told him that if he did not obey her she would grow worse instead of better. She saw him for ten minutes or a quarter of an hour before dinner, and then sent him away, pleading headache or sleepiness.

Meanwhile, the condition of the child was improving every day, and soon the doctor declared that there need be no further cause for anxiety on its account. It was christened George Augustus Davenport. George was Cecilia's choice; Augustus was selected in compliment to a very much beloved uncle of the Stern family; and Mrs. Rayner announced with a great deal of emphasis that the darling should inherit the family name of Davenport. The sound of these names followed by the surname of Stern (pronounced always like the English novelist, no one ever dreaming of disclosing its German origin by a conscientious adherence to the Frankfort pronunciation) produced a most satisfactory state of mind in Mrs. Rayner. It tickled her sense of the magnificent; and, half unconsciously, she associated the names with paragraphs she read in the "Times," concerning the movements of crowned heads and their families.

To Albert the child was a fresh justification of himself, just as his marriage with Cecilia had seemed to him to destroy his old conviction that he was a superfluous creature. He dreamed even more fervently than most fathers of all that his son would be. All the triumphs that ill health, circumstances, or the perverseness of fate had hindered the father from accomplishing were to be realised by the son. During the ten minutes which he spent with Cecilia every evening, until she was well enough to leave her bed, he never talked of anything else. Sometimes he even forgot to ask how she was, and began at once to describe some gesture or sound that he had observed the infant make. Cecilia, over whose eyelids always stole an increased pain when her husband entered the room, lay back on her pillows and gazed at him with half shut eyes. For several months she saw little of her child; its presence disturbed her; its cries made her nervous and ill at ease. She listened to the father's raptures with an air of long-suffering martyrdom upon her face, which sometimes changed to an expression of deeper resentment when the sight of his greasy black curls and the specks of scurf upon his coat offended her more than usual. Sometimes she would forget to answer questions which he addressed to her; and Albert, noticing the far-away look on her face, would ask, in a voice that showed that he was hurt, if she had heard what he said, or if she did not feel well again; and then she would complain of pains in her eyes, and say that she would try and sleep a little. She did not leave her bed until the middle of February, and Albert marked his gratitude at her improvement by filling the room with flowers; but after a little while she felt the perfume to be too strong, so they were removed.

She began now to see dressmakers, and order a quantity of clothes, over the making of which she spent hours of thought, planning out all the details in her head, and then talking them over with the nurse. She ordered fresh underlinen, as she declared that she could not bear anything but silk next her skin after her illness.

One day late in April, she sat in the sitting-room next her bedroom, and looked out into the square. It was one of those spring

Cecilia

days that seem to clothe London in a sudden beauty, as if by magic. The winter had been dull, sometimes cold, and always ugly. To-day the sky was a mild blue, and a mist hung over the square, behind which the opposite houses emerged here and there, looking like fragments of some fairy city. At four o'clock Cecilia told the nurse to go out, as she felt quite well enough to be left alone, and she sat in a soft, loose dress, covered with lace, opposite the window and looked out. There were green buds in the square, and the sound of traffic reached Cecilia's ears very faintly. Soon the beauty of the day penetrated into her so deeply that she rose languidly from her chair and opened the French window. The noise grew slightly louder, and a soft air floated into the room, blowing the hair about her face as she stood leaning against the window frame. She could feel the lace on her dress flutter and fall. A sparrow flew past her, twittering as it went, and a tenderness born of the physical delights of convalescence and the grace of the day stole over Cecilia, so that she thought for the first time with pleasure of her child, wondered what it was doing at that moment, and then, with a swift step, she made her way to the door, opened it, and listened. She fancied she heard the child upstairs, making a faint droning sound, but everywhere else the house was quiet. Then she stole up the stairs, pausing now and then to take fresh breath. She could feel her heart beat strongly, as her feverish fingers met the cool handle of the door. Then she opened it gently and looked in. Leaning against a pile of cushions cast recklessly upon the floor, the child sat up, and held out both its tiny hands, closing the fingers convulsively and opening them again, while its eyes stared in front of it at a large coloured ball which was rolling towards it. A few paces off Albert lay with his head in his hands, his face absorbed in watching the movements of

maternal

the little creature, so that for a moment he did not notice the entrance of Cecilia. The nurse was in an adjoining room, washing tea-cups, which clinked occasionally.

"I did n't hear you come in," said Cecilia, slowly. His presence shattered at once all the secret joy that she had been unconsciously promising herself from a few minutes alone with the child.

"I have been in about twenty minutes," said Albert, rising from the floor. "Is n't he a darling?" he went on, pointing to the child; but Cecilia did not answer his question.

"And instead of coming to see me, you came up here," she said bitterly.

"I thought you would be lying down, and I did n't want to disturb you."

"I was all alone in the sitting-room. At last I was afraid I might faint, and so I struggled up here. I sent nurse Alice out: it was not her fault. Oh, never mind," she went on, seeing that he was going to excuse himself, "it does n't matter; only I don't think I ought to have come upstairs alone, I feel so exhausted."

"Why did n't you ring for the maid?" he said, as he helped her clumsily to a chair.

"Oh, I give trouble enough!"

He brought the child to her for a caress. But she told him to take it to the nurse, as she was not strong enough at the moment. When he came back, she was wiping the sleeve of her dress, over which the child had dribbled, as he held it to her to kiss. When he offered to help her, she pushed him away, and went on muttering to herself over the stain on her sleeve.

"It's not the child's fault," he said at last.

"Ah, that's what I expected!" she burst out; "now take the child's part. Everything now is 'the child.' The child can't do wrong. The child must have this; the child must have that. Everything is to be upset for the child."

"Cecilia," he remonstrated.

Cecilia

"Yes, I tell you that the child is becoming a curse, — yes, a curse," she went on, seeing on his face the pain that she was inflicting by the word. "You spend all your time with it. It does n't matter what I am doing. You come up here, and sprawl on the floor, as if you were the mother, and whine over the child."

His voice was smothered in anger and emotion, as he replied:

"If you were to spend more time with your child, and take more interest in it, I should not be here so often."

"Oh, it 's easy enough for you to be sentimental over it! What have you had to suffer? You can afford to rejoice. It has cost you nothing." She burst into tears.

He was inconsolable, offered all the apologies that he could think of, protested that she wronged him; but for some time she would not listen to him, begged him only to leave her alone, until, wearied with her own vehemence, she allowed him to defend himself, to explain

266

what he had imagined she would feel to her child. He suggested that her life had been saved by a divine Providence, that her suffering had been sanctified, but she only smiled incredulously at him, and made her usual retort.

"Ah, Albert, how little you understand a woman."

As a last resort she always took refuge behind this reproach, coupling it with an air of magnanimous pardon for having made her so unhappy.

As the time slipped by, he was forced to content himself with attributing the state of her mind to the depression consequent upon her illness; and while he tried to believe that when she was quite restored to health her love for the child would shoot forth strong and tender, there was something in her eyes, as she lay in easy chairs about the room, which seemed to indicate a perpetual sense of injury, — almost as if some wrong had been done to her which could not be repaired.

V

As Cecilia grew stronger, she became more difficile, and contrived to bring about scenes with her husband more frequently. And, although they were always followed by a reconciliation, they nurtured a queer feeling of reserve between the two, to which, at least, Albert had hitherto been a stranger. He began to realise that there were many things "that a woman cannot understand," and he was compelled to acknowledge that, though the importance of sex was generally exaggerated by people, yet there was some foundation for their beliefs. He would occasionally explain to a friend how it was impossible to explain certain things to his wife, because she would never allow herself to envisage the possibility of understanding them, but would exercise a privileged unreasonableness, against which a man was powerless.

Cecilia

He spent more time than before outside his house; for he found that when he was at home too frequently, and for too long periods at a time, he was beset by endless small contretemps, under which he chafed. To whatever he proposed, Cecilia found some obstacle, — usually quite trifling, — but just sufficient to serve effectually as a bar to the execution of his intentions. Moreover, she told him frankly that his place was not at home during the day; for it was impossible for her to look after her house and her child if he was constantly requiring her presence. Besides, a man should have an occupation. She was ashamed that other people should see him tied to her apron strings all day. It looked foolish. She would not have people think that it was her wish. She induced him to join several clubs, that he might have a resort outside the house, where he would be sure of meeting friends. She forbade him to go into the nursery to see the little George; he must ring the bell and send for the child.

Cecilia

The servants would laugh at him if he were always romping on the floor; and the nurse would object to his invasion of the nursery, which, in all well-conducted houses, was never entered by the master of the house, and rarely by the mistress. By inventing arbitrary rules of this kind, which he had not the courage to disregard or dispute, she succeeded in securing her own way in everything that took place within the house. When Albert rebelled, which was seldom enough, she contrived to throw a suggestion of impropriety, almost of indelicacy over his objections, as if his conduct showed a brutal disregard for the feelings and instincts of a woman. When she had completely dressed herself in an armour of punctilio, and found that after a few idle remonstrances Albert acquiesced, she was still not satisfied.

She wanted to encounter resistance and contradiction from the man from whom every day she grew more estranged. She won her victories over him so easily, that they afforded her no satisfaction, and she was the more incensed against him that in the end his good nature, and a deep-rooted, wildly ideal faith in his wife, were proof against all the weapons of her contempt.

Once when he was late, and she had to wait five minutes for him, she grew very angry, and, without meaning him to take literally what she said, told him that whenever they made an appointment he ought to be there ten minutes before the time, — that it was his duty to wait for her, — and on the next occasion she discovered that he had obeyed her to the letter. She laughingly told him that, as he had repented properly, she would be content if the next time he were at the meeting place punctually at the time appointed. But, to her surprise and vexation, he persisted in waiting for her, "so as to be quite sure that she should not have to wait for him," and she had to grow angry again before he would give up the habit; and when his submissiveness left her again in the wrong, she was so angered that she cried in an exasperated voice:

"You have no sense of humour," which happened to be a just reproach.

Cecilia shut her eyes to the future, and went on living from day to day. She instinctively stopped herself from thinking, as much as she could. Every morning she spent longer over dressing, and grew more capricious in her choice of garments. She ordered hairdressers to come in to arrange her hair in different fashions; and, instead of the simple dresses which she wore before her marriage, she chose materials with elaborate designs of strange colours. But, in spite of all that she did, the truth gradually gained hold of her, that she had changed. Every morning that she looked into the glass the sight of the two dark rims round her eyes disgusted her. She took tonics and medicines, used glycerine and ointments for the skin; but nothing was of any avail. She would even put powder round her eyes, and brush it lightly off with a soft puff, leaving just sufficient for the blackness of these marks not to be visible. When she resumed her days at home, she ordered the blinds to be pulled half down, saying that the sunlight pained her eyes.

Albert's affection for the child grew stronger every day; but he indulged it in secret, and talked little to Cecilia about it, fearing that it would annoy her, and that she would misunderstand it. He still visited the nursery, but took good care that his wife should not know it, choosing his opportunities when she was out, or engaged. He realised the logic of her argument, when she complained of all the pain and discomfort that the child had caused her; but he felt that her sentiment which allowed her to express it was a crooked one. Still too loyal to the ideal view of his wife to openly condemn it, he suffered himself only to regret it as a circumstance for which no one could be held responsible.

As the summer advanced, Cecilia began to

entertain her friends, frequently gave dinner-parties and " At homes," and it was even noticed that she seldom talked to her husband in the presence of strangers. Albert had little to say as to the dates of these entertainments, or the people who were to be asked. Although Cecilia always consulted him on all these subjects, she did so in a way that left him no opportunity for exercising his own will.

One day towards the end of July, she told her husband that she had asked a number of people to dinner in the evening, and when he looked surprised that she had not told him before, said that the matter had escaped her memory. He was hurt by her indifference, but forbore to quarrel, as he realised that he would be powerless to convince Cecilia of a wanton disregard for him in a matter which she would persist in thinking of, and treating, as of minor importance.

He came home at about five o'clock, — hot, tired, and discontented. He was ill disposed to see a crowd of people that night, and would have preferred to be left alone; but that was not allowed him, and though he tried hard to put himself in the wrong, he could not help feeling aggrieved.

True, after her illness it was only natural that Cecilia would want relaxation, gaiety, the enjoyment of society; but why had she not told him? Had he ever refused her anything? He stole upstairs into the nursery to while away an hour with his child, for whom he had bought yet another toy, in spite of Cecilia's constant warning that he was spoiling the child beyond all chance of reparation, with his numerous presents. She even reproached him with that weakness to which she owed her own supremacy in the house.

The little George was now nine months old, and his father spent hours trying to make him speak, and building toy-houses for him. While he went up to play with him, Cecilia was already commencing an elaborate toilette in which she was to appear to receive her guests. Just as Albert had put the top brick to a fancy palace which he had reared on a board set up against the wall in lieu of a table for the child to play upon, the drawing-room clock struck half-past six, and the sound of the chimes floated up through the open doors into the room where the little George was gaping with wonder at the beautiful building that his father had raised. The sound caused a perplexed look to flit over the child's face, and Albert, catching the little creature in his arms, and holding him now high in the air, and now down upon the floor, cried, " Ding, dong, ding, dong, ding, dong," until the smooth skin of the child's face puckered into endless wrinkles, and it, too, began to make a sound like " ding, dong," and to coo with delight as it flew up and down in the arms of its father. But he had to leave it to go and dress for dinner; and then it cried with rage, whilst Albert felt pained at the sudden change from laughter to tears, and was not too well disposed when the guests began to arrive. Several times during dinner he addressed a question to his wife across the table; but she never heard him, and continued to talk with her neighbour, a friend of Albert's, a barrister, who had come to his house for the first time, and was charmed with the appearance and fascinating manners of Cecilia. She ate little dinner, but looked very handsome as she talked with this young man, and lazily waved a large white feather fan to and fro in front of her.

For the first time since her illness she consented to play the piano, at the repeated request of the young barrister; and the brilliantly lighted room echoed with applause as she raised her jewelled hand from the keyboard at the close of what she called a phantasia of Godard, although the greater part of it was a fancy of her own, which she composed with much skill as she went along.

entertaining gentleman / attention on her beauty.

Cecilia

When everybody had left, and Cecilia, at the open window, had watched the last carriage drive away, she was about to leave the room, when Albert asked her to stay and talk for a few minutes.

"What do you want?" she said wearily.

"Only to admire you a little, now that every one else has gone."

"Are n't you tired of doing that?" she said, as she watched the grease forming patterns down the sides of the candles in sconces on the walls, as the summer air floated through the window and made the flames flicker.

"Cecilia, how beautiful you look, and how well you played to-night!"

"I'm tired; can't you see it in my face? Why don't you let me go to bed?"

"Play something to me — anything you like — and then I won't keep you any longer."

"Play? Now? Why, everybody's gone! How unkind of you to keep me chattering when I tell you I'm tired!"

278

Cecilia

"You were n't tired when some one else asked you to play," he said a little bitterly.

"Ah," she broke out, "jealous! I thought so! You think you alone have a right to admire me because I am your wife. But you will have to allow other people to admire. Besides, what have I done that you should say such things to me? What have I done, I say?"

She went on, raising her voice defiantly as he kept silence.

"Because I have talked to some one else and played a piece on the piano to — to —" she could not find a word suitable to her statement of the case, "to save the expense of hiring musicians," she said at last, "I am to be reproached and made unhappy."

"Cecilia, you know that is not what I mean. You know that I never deny you anything; that I give you all that you ask."

"Presents!" she screamed, "presents! You can have them back, all of them!" and she

Cecilia

tore from her neck a string of diamonds, and flung them on the ground. He had given them to her on her wedding day. "Take them! take them!" she went on, her voice choking with anger, "only leave me alone!" and she buried her face in her hands and fled from the room, leaving him dazed and wounded, while the necklace lay coiled at his feet, gleaming here and there where the light of the candles fell upon the stones.

VI

THE next day Albert went to the Temple as usual, and Cecilia did not rise till late. In the afternoon Aubrey Melville called in Berkeley Square for the first time since the marriage. His notoriety had rather waned since his appearance as a prominent citizen among a crowd of insurgents at the St. James's Theatre. He still preserved a cadaverous and interesting appearance, and a walk that was known, amongst the members of the Parish Dramatic Club of which Cecilia and he had once been distinguished members, as "The Melville."

Cecilia heard the announcement of his name with considerable pleasure. She installed him comfortably in an easy chair, and then seated herself opposite him, intending to settle down to a long conversation.

Cecilia

Melville, his head slightly on one side, asked her, in a hollow voice, which was in excellent harmony with his cadaverous appearance, how she liked married life?

"Oh, it has many advantages!" said Cecilia, rather absently. She was looking at him and reconstructing in her mind the events that preceded her marriage.

He admired her house, and suggested that she should sing something.

"Sing, my dear Aubrey? No, I have been so ill. Besides, there is no time for that now."

He apologised for forgetting that she had been ill, observed that he had noticed that she was pale, and added, by way of compliment, that there was compensation for her illness.

"Yes, and then to be living with the person one loves best in the world," Cecilia added, with all her former vivacity and address.

Mr. Melville was about to make a suitable reply, when the door was opened and the servant announced Mrs. Rayner.

Cecilia

Cecilia was vexed beyond measure at the interruption, the more so because she was compelled to treat it with the utmost outward complacence. Mrs. Rayner positively sailed into the room, in a black velvet mantle heavily trimmed with jet, and a bonnet from which sprang a couple of orange aigrettes.

"My darling Cecilia, how are you, my child?" she cried, as she clasped the accommodating Cecilia in her arms, and kissed her fervently. Then she turned to the young man. "I never see you now, Mr. Melville. Now that my child has left me, now that I am a grandmother, no one calls on me." She did not wait for an apology, but turned again to Cecilia.

"Where is the joy of joys?" she said.

"If you mean the boy Gussie," said Cecilia, with a ring of slight contempt in her voice, "he is out, — or at least he was out. Perhaps he is back by now." She went to the bell, which was almost immediately answered by the servant, whom she instructed to find out if the nurse had come back, and if so, to tell her to bring the baby into the drawing-room.

In a few moments, which were occupied in exchanging commonplaces, the door opened and the nurse and child appeared, both dressed for out-doors. They had come straight in, without staying to remove their wraps.

Mrs. Rayner at once flew into the wildest ecstasies. She talked the most amazing language to the child, which lay in the arms of its nurse, with a cold, indifferent stare in its vacant little eyes. She danced round it, adopting the interrogative form of address, and asking it an infinity of questions, which followed one another in rapid and inconsequent succession. She preserved her own dignity and that of the infant, by talking to it in the third person.

" Has it been out, the little George ? Has it got its best white frock on — its very best white frock ? " and she bobbed backwards and forwards ; " and does it feel proud of its fine white hat; yes, white hat, beautiful white hat, white hat, white hat," she went on, in depressing reiteration.

Something in the eyebrows of Cecilia denoted a patient, long-suffering submission to her mother's idiosyncrasies, as she went on talking to Aubrey Melville, in ostensible indifference to the presence of the baby. She asked the young man about himself. What had he been doing? How was he getting on in his profession? Aubrey answered mechanically, somewhat disconcerted by the noises that proceeded from the other end of the room, where the little George, wearied at his grandmother's aggressive attempts to insinuate herself into his good graces, began to frown and dart distress out of his round eyes.

" He wants his mother," cried Mrs. Rayner. "Of course he wants his mother. Why don't you come to him, Cecilia, and show Mr. Melville what a monster he is?"

Cecilia rose, with a look of resignation, and

Cecilia

Aubrey followed her respectfully to the group at the other end of the room. No sooner had they joined her, than Mrs. Rayner, satisfied that they had come, began to resume her coquetteries, and even asked Melville a number of questions which she neither expected nor intended he should answer. At last she paused, feeling that the appropriate moment had arrived for the mother to take the reins of affection from her hands. Cecilia, too, felt that some evidence of maternal interest was expected of her, but her mother's conduct had roused her sense of ridicule.

She looked queerly at the little creature who was sitting up in the nurse's arms now, and gazing fixedly at her. Roughly pushing away the little hat made of broad white ribbon and white lace, until it half tumbled over the child's forehead, she burst into a peal of laughter at the grotesqueness of his appearance, and asked Melville if he did n't look a tipsy baby?

Cecilia

Melville acquiesced, with an awkward laugh which indicated pretty clearly that he was embarrassed; but Mrs. Rayner interposed, adopted a grand attitude as defender of her grandchild's dignity, and righted the little hat, with many compassionate and endearing terms. She then took an effusive leave of her daughter, alleging that she had positively promised to call on Lady Bland, and did not dare to disappoint her, much as she would have liked to stay a little longer with the dear child. Cecilia would have kept Melville for further conversation, but he pleaded an early rehearsal, and took his leave, first seeing Mrs. Rayner into a hired brougham which was waiting outside. The orange aigrettes played out of the window at him as the long-limbed horse settled at once into a mechanical, stiff-kneed trot in the direction of Belgravia.

Cecilia stood still and listened to the sound of the wheels as it grew fainter and fainter, and at last died away in the vague roar of the

Cecilia

traffic. Then she turned and walked wearily across the room. She was just going to sink into a chair, when the reflected image of her face in a mirror aroused her curiosity, and she stood looking at herself.

The heat of the day was just beginning to decline, and through the lower half of the windows, which was not covered by the blinds, came a full rich light which bathed all the furniture of the room in a warm colour. A large bluebottle buzzed and scrambled over the window pane, walking over and over again up the glass until he met the wooden frame, when he burst into circles and hit his body again and again against the window, with a queer dull sound, until he relapsed into silence and began once more to crawl up from the bottom.

Cecilia passed her hand over her face. Still the black rings round the eyes; and she gazed into them as she stroked the lids and passed her fingers round the soft skin in a circle.

Cecilia

How the beauty of her youth had faded.
The face before her seemed hard and ugly,—
yes, ugly. Her illness had left marks that
were indelible. Was this what her marriage
meant? Was she to grow uglier and uglier
from day to day? Why had not Aubrey
Melville yielded to her persuasion to stay a
little longer? That would never have been
the case in the old days. Yes, that was it:
she was growing dull, uninteresting. And was
there no escape? Soon he would be home
again, her husband, and she must smile and
look pleased, and ask him to forgive her for
her cruelty of the night before, forgive her
—forgive. Why should she ask forgiveness? Had she not suffered enough? Then
she remembered saying once to Aubrey Melville, when he had teased her for not getting
married, "I should be a terrible person:
nothing would ever keep me with a man
whom I had ceased to love."

And the bluebottle buzzed on the window

pane, dancing and sputtering and fizzing in a
frenzy of baffled rage as he encountered the
wooden rim for the hundredth time.

"Nothing would ever keep me with a man
I had ceased to love." And her mind
wandered back to the time before her marriage.
Then at least her body was undefiled, and the
pride of her beauty untainted. Now even
that was corrupt. Her eyes ached with staring
so long at the reflection of her face in the
glass. She closed them for a moment, and
when she looked into them again the pain and
melancholy in them frightened her.

"Nothing would ever keep me with a man
whom I have ceased to love," — the words
would not leave her. They seemed to beat
against the sides of her head. A helpless
wonder passed through her mind as she
thought of the love that other mothers were
supposed to have for their children.

Suddenly the sharp cry of the little George,
which reached her from upstairs, jarred so

violently upon her nerves that the stream of her discontent, which had been growing larger and larger, swept over her and bore down everything before it. Hitherto, her resistance had been passive, a silent rebellion of spirit. Now the plaintive cry of the child stung her to action.

Albert Stern came home dull and tired. The smell of the law courts, the rasping voice of the lawyer, the heat and the noise of the streets had all contributed to his disgust. The pain which Cecilia's conduct on the night before had inflicted on him still rankled in him. They had not spoken since she had flung from the room and cast at his feet the necklace which he had given her as a wedding present. He knew that she would ask his forgiveness; and the fact that she was in the wrong pained him, so that he hastened to get this reconciliation over, and, though observing a stillness in the house as he closed the door behind him, did not stop to account for it, but hurried upstairs, leaving his hat and stick in the hall.

The door of the drawing-room was open, and was swinging gently to and fro in the wind that swept through the open window. When he entered the room he found it empty. He wandered about aimlessly. The tea-tray was upon a little table near the mantel-piece, and had not been taken down by the servant. A letter was slipped between the cups which Albert supposed was intended for the post. His belief was strengthened when he recognised in the address the handwriting of Cecilia, and he was just about to put it back in its place, when he fancied it was addressed to himself. Taking it to the window where the bluebottle was still climbing up the pane, and pulling up the blind, he was surprised to find his suspicions confirmed. Slowly opening the envelope, as if he were ashamed to be seen, he read, in his wife's bold handwriting:

Cecilia

I have gone away, you will never know where, and don't try and understand why, because you cannot. I could not have been any use to you in the long run, and you will get on perfectly well without me.

CECILIA.

He stood helplessly with the note in his hand, vainly trying to realise what the words meant. Then instinctively he rushed to the nursery, where he found his little son sprawling on the floor; and when he went to kiss him, the child put his fist in his face and cried, "Mamma!" Albert.

As he hastened downstairs again, he wanted to call out with all his might "Cecilia;" but the sound stuck in his throat, and the thought of making inquiries of the servants passed idly through his head without his being able to translate it into action. He took his hat and stick and hurried into the street, not knowing where he was going, feeling only that he must move about.

293

Cecilia

For hours and hours he wandered along, deceived every moment by the dress or the walk of some woman into believing that she must be his wife. Clusters of stars appeared in the sky, and all the beauty of a midsummer night burst upon London. The streets echoed with the shouts of little children at play; men and women walked arm in arm along the pavements. And while the heart of the great city throbbed with the feverish gaiety of the last few days of the season, and the glamour of the stars fell from overhead upon the houses, the lights, the men and women who swarmed everywhere like clouds of insects, Albert Stern wandered far away, down unknown streets, through countless labyrinths, past public houses from which came the noise of tavern music mixed with coarse laughter and song, dazed and stricken with a pain in his chest that gnawed like a wound.

And when at last he found himself again in Berkeley Square, the dawn had begun to glimmer, and a great sleep had fallen upon the city, and the air was still. At an open doorway stood a young man and a girl in evening dress, while at the further end of the hall were gathered a group of people. The lights were still burning in the house, and it could be seen that the dance had come to an end.

"You are certain you will never regret it," said the young man, earnestly. The girl only bowed her head and answered in a whisper, "I am certain;" and he kissed her lightly on the forehead.

And as Albert passed, his wound seemed deeper than ever. He was tormented by the sensation of a soft silk sleeve rubbing against his arm, as in the days when he and Cecilia used to walk together. Famished and weary underfoot, he crept into his house and sat alone at the dining-room window in the old place which he had taken when Cecilia was so ill; and he stared out at the blank road, while

Cecilia

the light grew stronger and stronger, until the birds began to carol as the first beam of sunlight fell from the sky and touched with a tender glory the city of leaves that trembled in the square.

Epilogue

I

JUST as the story falls by itself into three parts, so does it seem inevitable that the author should set out arguments to justify the making of a fourth, which he is pleased to call an epilogue, as well as a certain grave omission of details closely concerning Cecilia herself.

And for the epilogue a defence is found in the author's fear that, were the story to be ended with the third part, the reader might suffer his fancy to drive Cecilia to a false conclusion, either by drowning her in her own tears of repentance, or by raising her to undue heights of ill-won prosperity. And if there be any to whom a conclusion different from either of these must be a disappointment, they would do well to lay aside the book at once.

Cecilia

When we leave a space of time or a set of events undefined, we put ourselves at the mercy of the reader ; we pray that his imagination may be fired by what has gone before, and that so our silence may be made eloquent. Much might be written of Cecilia's adventures soon after her flight ; it is to be feared that an account of them, while satisfying the reader's curiosity, might distort his vision. But enough — to attempt to justify an omission is to confess ourselves in the wrong, so let us on and take our chance.

" Two years ? " said Mrs. Sherbetter, incredulously, as she sat in Miss Savory's drawing-room on a hot summer afternoon. She had outstayed all the other visitors.

" I can't believe it," she went on ; "why it seems only yesterday that I was here after driving in the park — don't you remember, Miss Savory ? I had seen them dash past in a victoria, and they certainly did n't look very happy then — but it can't be two whole years already since it all happened," and Mrs. Sherbetter put her hand to the back of her soft, silky knob of hair, and smiled at herself in several of Miss Savory's looking-glasses.

"Two years," said Miss Savory, emphatically, with a slightly peevish ring in her voice which indicated that she would rather talk more about the Sterns and less about Mrs. Sherbetter's impressions.

"And nothing has been heard of poor Cecilia since that terrible evening?"

"Nothing," replied Miss Savory, mysteriously and grandly. On this occasion Miss Savory did not cluck. She only gazed in front of her, and blinked with her clear, baby-like eyes. There was a pause for a few moments in the conversation. Then Mrs. Sherbetter, with a desperate attempt at indifference, while she played with the lace round her parasol, asked in a discreet voice:

"With whom did she run off?"

"Who run off?" said Miss Savory, with an impenetrable stare.

"Poor Cecilia," said Mrs. Sherbetter, humbly.

"She ran away by herself," replied Miss Savory, in a calm, unmoved voice which suggested that this was only a very small portion of the information which she could give if she chose.

Mrs. Sherbetter was terribly perplexed. She had not anticipated such a reply. She quite expected to hear that Cecilia had been ruined by Aubrey Melville, or a musician with long hair who played divinely. She murmured respectfully :

"Oh, impossible! What could have induced her to run away from a beautiful house, every comfort, a sweet child?"

The want of worldly precaution involved in such conduct was unintelligible to her. She never dreamed of the possibility of any woman, however unhappy, leaving her home, unless she could fly into the substantial arms of a sympathetic lover.

This time there was a longer pause, to which Mrs. Sherbetter at last put an end by rising with a pretence of going, which made Miss Savory relent a little for her stern want of communicativeness.

" How is poor Mrs. Rayner ? " asked Mrs. Sherbetter, when she had seated herself again at the request of Miss Savory. She sounded decidedly bolder than in the early part of the conversation.

" She will never get over it. Her nerves are shattered, positively shattered." Miss Savory liked the word shattered; so she repeated it several times to herself. " If the dear girl had only consulted her," she went on, " before taking such a grave step, everything might have been well. But to go away without leaving her address. To leave everybody, even her mother, for two whole years in an agony of suspense —"

" I always thought Cecilia a very queer

girl," added Mrs. Sherbetter, by way of filling in a difficult gap.

"If we only now knew where she was," continued Miss Savory, "we could bring an action for divorce."

Mrs. Sherbetter was again completely at a loss to understand.

"Mrs. Rayner has proofs that Albert Stern was a wicked husband, — a very cruel, wicked husband. She swore it to me the other day, with tears in her eyes, — don't repeat what I say," added Miss Savory, suddenly resuming her august manner.

A light began to glimmer in the mind of Mrs. Sherbetter. Until now, with all the best intentions in the world to be as malicious as possible, it had not occurred to her that Albert Stern might be guilty in the matter; but she realised how necessary it was for Miss Savory to adopt this version, if she did not wish to appear disloyal to her old friend.

Evading a direct reply, "Do you know I

always thought the husband a little funny," she said, " as if he were not quite right in his mind ? "

It was a masterly remark. To take up any side in the matter would have been fatal ; for, if she had entirely agreed with Miss Savory, the conversation would in all probability have come to an immediate end, whilst, if she had disagreed, she would have made the old lady extremely angry. The suggestion that Albert Stern was a lunatic seemed to change the whole aspect of the case from one of scandal to that of disaster. Who could blame a wife for running away from a madman ? Who could blame a husband for deeds for which it was impossible to hold him responsible ? Moreover, the novelty of the suggestion stimulated the loquacity of Miss Savory.

" Whether he was mad or not before his marriage may be a matter of conjecture — but he certainly behaved very madly after his wife had left him."

Cecilia

"Indeed!" said Mrs. Sherbetter, compassionately.

"They say that for two months he never spoke," continued Herminia. "No doubt he was afraid of saying something to his own discredit; but he looked paler and uglier than ever. On the morning after she had left him, they found him half asleep in the dining-room, and on the floor was a letter which he had begun to his brother, in which he confessed that *it was all his own fault*; so you see there can be no doubt of his guilt," she added severely. "Then they sent him on a voyage round the world to restore his health, or to allow time enough to pass for the affair to be forgotten before he appeared again in society."

"And what became of the dear little child?"

"The David Sterns took it. It grows every day more and more like its father, — a monster, a perfect monster with a Jew nose," said Miss Savory, working herself into a passion.

"And has Mr. Stern, the young Mr. Stern, I mean, come back yet from his travels?"

"I believe he came back last month; but I never see him. Neither I nor Mrs. Rayner will consent to have anything more to do with the Stern family."

"I suppose the house in Berkeley Square was sold," said Mrs. Sherbetter, rising to take her leave.

"The house in Berkeley Square *was* sold," said Miss Savory, looking very enigmatical indeed; but Mrs. Sherbetter's thirst for information was quenched, and she tripped lightly towards the door, her silk dress rustling as she walked. And in recognition of the confidence that Miss Savory had reposed in her, she admired an engraving of "The Lord's Supper," which hung on the walls of the little hall into which she stepped, and even threw a kiss to her hostess from the tip of her gloved fingers, as the servant closed the front door behind her.

II

I⟨T⟩ was a gala night at the Trois Etoiles, Place
des Ternes. The chandeliers on the first floor
were alight, a circumstance which in itself
indicated that the occasion was a festive one,
for Madame was renowned for her economy.

The ground floor of the house was a restaurant of the third-rate order in Paris. You
could get an excellent dinner with wine included for three francs; but it was as well not
to examine the table-cloth, or the knives and
forks, too closely. The chief business was
done in absinthe and beer, drunk at little round
marble tables set out upon the pavement.

The first floor consisted of a small boarding-
house establishment, over which Madame herself presided, and from which she contrived to
make sufficient money to live in comfort with
an occasional extravagance. One of these ex-
travagances was a dinner which she gave every

fortnight to the other inhabitants of the floor, followed by a dance, at which everybody became very gay before the evening came to an end. People often went up from the café below, it being generally understood that every second Wednesday Madame entertained.

A placard with the words *Jour de fête* was hung round the neck of a plaster figure which surmounted each column under the portico at the entrance to the restaurant. These figures represented the lower half of a fish, and the bust and head of a woman whose head was crowned with three gilt stars, which gave the name to the restaurant. Regular clients never required to look at these placards; for the illumination of the room on the first floor, which could be seen from the street, was a swifter means of communication.

Besides, the house was well known in the neighbourhood.

The phrase *aux trois étoiles* had even acquired a peculiar signification among the local shopkeepers. It meant "on the spree," "in the seventh heaven of debauchery," so that when the grocer's wife inquired after the health of "Papa Victor" as she sat gossiping at the post-office with Madame Victor, and that good-natured, fat lady answered with a shrug of her broad, amiable shoulders, "Que voulez-vous, il est toujours aux trois étoiles," she meant that her husband was constantly committing fresh excesses, possibly at the café in the Place, but at numerous other places besides.

On this evening, "Papa Victor" was enjoying himself hugely. He was seated at Madame's hospitable table by the side of a little music-hall singer, who was constantly humming one of her songs and tapping with her finger on the table to mark the rhythm. "Papa Victor" imitated her example, putting his thick finger also upon the table and following the tune in an ecstasy of delight which spread itself all over his face. The singer was dressed in a marvellous arrangement of white satin ribbons, in which she was going to sing afterwards at the El Dorado. On her left hand sat a young poet who was writing a volume of verses of which no one had as yet heard anything but the title, which was " Sighs from the Cradle." Once he had begun to recite the first line of a sonnet at the end of dinner, but he was greeted with such a shout of laughter that he sat down, and never again alluded to his profession.

A dancing mistress who taught the most distinguished families in every quarter of Paris, as you could read on the brass plate of her door, was also present on this evening. She had brought with her a daughter, and a favourite pupil who was one day going to astonish the world. These, with three French students and an old jeweller whose premises were beneath those of the dancing mistress, made up the party.

It was a very rowdy evening. The best wines had been served in great profusion, and the conversation, which was animated and had divided itself up amongst couples, was broken here and there by the noise of laughter and the rattle of the china upon the table.

All of a sudden, the hostess, who was exquisitely dressed in pink and grey silk, rose and tried to attract the attention of the rest at the table, but no one would listen. "Papa Victor" was talking fast to the little singer, and trying to remember a song he had heard when he was a boy,—a song of which the refrain was—he scratched his head and muttered helplessly to himself. The dancing mistress was engaged in demonstrating a figure in a new dance which she had invented, and which she indicated by dipping a toothpick in the dregs of her wine and drawing a picture on the table-cloth, and the students were paying the younger ladies an earnest attention, when at last Madame took up a fork and tapped loudly with it on a metal centre-piece which was filled with sweetmeats. There was a burst of laughter and everybody followed suit. "Papa Victor" could not find a fork, amid the confusion of the table, so he dexterously pulled off the white satin slipper of his neighbour and beat a tattoo with it on the centre-piece. The noise was deafening; then some one cried, " Silence pour la patronne," and the clamour subsided.

Madame herself was now seized with a fit of laughter which occasioned titters of sympathy round the table, until at last she announced that dancing would now begin in the next room. A loud huzza burst from the guests as they rose and crowded round her, with their glasses in their hands, and drank her health. When she had accepted this testimony to her popularity with much grace, the party went into the next room, in which a jangling piano and a strident violin had already begun to sound.

Meanwhile, the opening night of the winter opera season in Paris had been very brilliant, and Prince Pezarin did not regret that he had taken a ticket, although it was at least the hundredth time that he saw " Faust " performed.

During the entr'acte, as he was walking up and down the foyer with Monsieur de Pommarion, he was perplexed by the face of a lady whom he remembered to have seen before, and who bowed graciously in response to his salutation. She was richly dressed, and wore a mass of jewels in her bodice and in her hair. He asked Monsieur de Pommarion if he knew who she was, and was agreeably relieved when his friend reminded him of Lady Killigrew, whom they had both known years ago in Emilienbad. They began to chat about the little German watering-place, and the Prince asked what had become of Dornstein. The wrinkled face of Monsieur de Pommarion seemed to grow more wrinkled, and his small sharp eyes to grow smaller, as he said that he believed that he recognised him in one of the croupiers, when he was at Monte Carlo a year ago.

Cecilia

The Prince grinned with a malicious satisfaction as the two separated, to return to their
seats for the last act. He was now reminded
more than ever of Dornstein by the music of
the opera, and he saw again in his mind the
scene in the concert-room of the Casino when
Dornstein had sung a duet with the accomplished Cecilia Rayner. He smiled as he
thought of the little Austrian raking in the
heaps of gold with a long black stick, and droning out the monotonous language of the rouge
et noir. And Cecilia? What had become of
her? Ah, he remembered, married to the
man with the sallow skin; and she passed out
of his mind as one who had become merged in
the commonplaces of life.

He left the opera-house humming the valse,
and, in spite of its being a cold night, walked
along, comfortably wrapped in a long, thick fur
coat which emphasised his natural height. He
felt thirsty after the heat of the theatre, but
passed by the cafés, too idle to interrupt the

pleasure he was taking from stretching his limbs after sitting in a cramped position during the last act of the performance. He was on his way to the Avenue de Villiers to see La Poussière, who had invited him to supper, when his attention was arrested by the brilliantly-lighted room of the Trois Etoiles, and he realised that he had gone a little too far. Feeling slightly fatigued, for he had now been walking rather more than half an hour, he entered the café and called for an absinthe. Certainly this was far too sordid a place for him to have visited in the ordinary course of events, for good living was one of the first principles of his life; but the brilliance of the windows above stimulated his curiosity. How came he not to have noticed this café before — he who prided himself on knowing every corner of Paris?

He engaged the waiter in conversation, and, writing a name on a slip of paper, sent him upstairs with it. On his return, the man offered to show the way to the company; and the Prince followed him up a narrow, carpetless staircase, and was shown into the dancing-room.

Madame was standing against the wall talking very quickly, and with many gestures, to the dancing mistress. " Papa Victor " and the little singer had gone ; but the party had been augmented by some visitors after dinner.

When the Prince saw Madame Cécile, his surprise was boundless. He began to talk to her in English ; but she answered him in French, called him her dear old friend, and thanked him repeatedly for coming to see her. She asked him if he cared to dance, and when he shook his head, led him into the next room, under pretext of making him drink a glass of excellent wine. As she passed on the arm of the Prince into the dining-room, she left open one of the folding doors which connected the two rooms. Pezarin was delighted with her. She was so engaging, and she looked wonderfully pretty.

Cecilia

"Come, sit down here," she said, "and we will watch the dancing; it looks charming from this spot," and she drew up two chairs to face the open door, and seating herself in one, lay back and half closed her eyes.

"What a long, long time ago it seems! Three — four — four or five years since, and you look just the same as ever — only handsomer, far handsomer, Pezarin. You were getting fat when we left Emilienbad. I made a remark about it to mamma."

"And you, Mademoiselle — pardon, Madame," he said, with an air of mock submission of which she took no notice.

"Well, what about me? Don't I look quite as pretty as I did then? What about the others?" she asked suddenly, and her face was convulsed with laughter as she inquired after Dornstein.

When the Prince had told her all he knew, she began to describe how Dornstein had come over to England on purpose to propose to her; and she acted over the whole scene in which she had taken part, until the Prince was so captivated that he could have kissed her. She stroked an imaginary beard as she represented the beginning of the interview. By the mimicry of her gestures, and the irritable look which she contrived to conjure into her eyes, she recalled to the mind of Pezarin the fiery temper for which Dornstein was notorious. She rose from her chair and stood in an attitude, as she impersonated the tragic Dornstein wounded in a fictitious duel in an unmentionable spot. When she had finished, the Prince positively cried with laughter.

In the meanwhile, the dancing party in the next room was diminishing. They left in couples, without bidding their hostess good-bye, but just glancing through the half-open door as they passed on their way out of the dancing-room.

"And you are happy?" said the Prince, breaking the silence that had risen between them, when they had both exhausted their laughter over the scene which she had acted.

" As happy as I ever was," she said with a little sigh, half spontaneous, half assumed.

The sound of closing doors reached them as they sat there, the noise of a man and a woman disputing, then the slamming of another door. The last couple passed out of the dancing-room, followed by the dancing mistress and the jeweller. The sound of their footsteps on the wooden staircase grew fainter and fainter; then all was still. The parquet floor still shone with the light reflected from the chandelier.

" Ah! Your husband must have been a sad dog," said the Prince, wishing to please her, "un très mauvais sujet," he repeated, observing that she was staring in front of her as if she had not heard his question.

" Who?" she said sharply, turning towards him.

" What was his name?" said the Prince,

with a puzzled look. He snapped his fingers as he tried to remember.

" An ugly little Jew was he not — Albert — Albert — "

" Don't let us talk about that, please," Cecilia answered, and her voice trembled. " You must not speak of him like that — You don't know — " She stopped and made an effort to smile.

The Prince saw that he had made a wrong move, and very shortly afterwards took his leave, murmuring to himself as he stepped into the cold air of the street, " How life repeats itself ! "

THE MIRROR OF MUSIC

SOME PRESS OPINIONS

"It is a new thing in literature. There is a magnificent breadth, a simple directness, about the conception of this diary, and the leading idea is worked out with a resourceful ingenuity, a piercing insight, and an unerring taste which betray the hand of some one very like a master." — *Woman.*

"A remarkably original and noteworthy book." — *Saturday Review.*

"A fantastic and original book, to which belongs that note of distinction rare in the days of crude and rapid production." — *Daily News.*

"The volume is a very remarkable one, and will be valued most of all by those who love music in its best and noblest forms." — *Western Morning News.*

"Has the unquestionable merit of novelty of conception." — *Daily Telegraph.*

"Strikes a very distinctive note of its own. There has never been a more daring and clever attempt in England at expression of emotion by music." — *Yorkshire Herald.*

"This truly marvellous book." — *Liverpool Mercury.*

"There have been few more striking revelations of the psychology of the musical temperament, and the writing is full of subtle beauty." — *Star.*

"As original in conception as it is admirable in execution. Narrated with a weird power that holds the reader breathless and almost horrified. Mr. Makower has certainly produced a remarkable work." — *Whitehall Review.*

"It is not too much to say that the language is beautiful, and that the study of a mind proceeding by stages from eccentricity to raving lunacy is most cleverly imagined." — *St. James's Gazette.*

"It is a very striking study of the phenomena of mental disease : and its power is enhanced by the fact that the sufferer is left to tell her own tale." — *Speaker.*

"There is a weird power in the study of insanity, of which the book consists, and the gradual transition from a state of high wrought excitement to one of absolute mania, is painted with remarkable skill." — *Morning Post.*

List of Books

IN

BELLES LETTRES

Published by John Lane

The Bodley Head

VIGO STREET, LONDON, W.

Adams (Francis).
ESSAYS IN MODERNITY. Crown 8vo. 5s. net. [*Shortly.*
A CHILD OF THE AGE. (*See* KEYNOTES SERIES.)

A. E.
HOMEWARD SONGS BY THE WAY. Sq. 16mo, wrappers. 1s. 6d. net. *Transferred to the present Publisher.* [*Second Edition.*
THE EARTH BREATH, AND OTHER POEMS. [*In preparation.*

Aldrich (T. B.)
LATER LYRICS. Sm. Fcap. 8vo. 2s. 6d. net.

Allen (Grant).
THE LOWER SLOPES: A Volume of Verse. With Title-page and Cover Design by J. ILLINGWORTH KAY. Crown 8vo. 5s. net.
THE WOMAN WHO DID. (*See* KEYNOTES SERIES.)
THE BRITISH BARBARIANS. (*See* KEYNOTES SERIES.)

Arcady Library (The).
A Series of Open-Air Books. Edited by J. S. FLETCHER. With Cover Designs by PATTEN WILSON. Each volume crown 8vo. 5s. net.
I. ROUND ABOUT A BRIGHTON COACH OFFICE. By MAUDE EGERTON KING. With over 30 Illustrations by LUCY KEMP-WELCH.
II. LIFE IN ARCADIA. By J. S. FLETCHER. With 20 Illustrations by PATTEN WILSON.

Arcady Library (The)—*cont.*
III. SCHOLAR GIPSIES. By JOHN BUCHAN. With 7 full-page Etchings by D.Y. CAMERON
IV. IN THE GARDEN OF PEACE. By HELEN MILMAN. With 24 Illustrations by EDMUND H. NEW.
V. THE HAPPY EXILE. By H. D. LOWRY. With 6 Etchings by E. PHILIP PIMLOTT. [*In preparation.*

Beeching (Rev. H. C.).
IN A GARDEN : Poems. With Title-page designed by ROGER FRY. Crown 8vo. 5s. net.
ST. AUGUSTINE AT OSTIA. Crown 8vo, wrappers. 1s. net.

Beerbohm (Max).
THE WORKS OF MAX BEERBOHM. With a Bibliography by JOHN LANE. Sq. 16mo. 4s. 6d. net.

Benson (Arthur Christopher)
LYRICS. Fcap. 8vo, buckram. 5s. net.
LORD VYET AND OTHER POEMS. Fcap. 8vo. 3s. 6d. net.

Bodley Head Anthologies (The).
Edited by ROBERT H. CASE. With Title-page and Cover Designs by WALTER WEST. Each volume crown 8vo. 5s. net.
I. ENGLISH EPITHALAMIES. By ROBERT H. CASE.

Bodley Head Anthologies (The)—*continued.*

II. MUSA PISCATRIX. By JOHN BUCHAN. With 6 Etchings by E. PHILIP PIMLOTT.

III. ENGLISH ELEGIES. By JOHN C. BAILEY.
[In preparation.

IV. ENGLISH SATIRES. By CHAS. HILL DICK.
[In preparation.

Bridges (Robert).

SUPPRESSED CHAPTERS AND OTHER BOOKISHNESS. Crown 8vo. 3s. 6d. net. *[Second Edition.*

Brotherton (Mary).

ROSEMARY FOR REMEMBRANCE. With Title-page and Cover Design by WALTER WEST. Fcap. 8vo. 3s. 6d. net.

Crackanthorpe (Hubert).

VIGNETTES. A Miniature Journal of Whim and Sentiment. Fcap. 8vo, boards. 2s. 6d. net.

Crane (Walter).

TOY BOOKS. Re-issue, each with new Cover Design and End Papers. This LITTLE PIG'S PICTURE BOOK, containing :
　I. THIS LITTLE PIG.
　II. THE FAIRY SHIP.
　III. KING LUCKIEBOY'S PARTY.

The three bound in one volume with a decorative cloth cover, end papers, and a newly written and designed preface and title-page. 3s. 6d. net ; separately 9d. net each.

MOTHER HUBBARD'S PICTURE BOOK, containing :
　I. MOTHER HUBBARD'S.
　II. THE THREE BEARS.
　III. THE ABSURD A. B. C.

The three bound in one volume with a decorative cloth cover, end papers, and a newly written and designed preface and title-page. 3s. 6d. net ; separately 9d. net each.

Custance (Olive).

OPALS : Poems. Fcap. 8vo. 3s. 6d. net.

Dalmon (C. W.).

SONG FAVOURS. With a Title-page by J. P. DONNE. Sq. 16mo. 3s. 6d. net.

Davidson (John).

PLAYS : An Unhistorical Pastoral ; A Romantic Farce ; Bruce, a Chronicle Play ; Smith, a Tragic Farce ; Scaramouch in Naxos, a Pantomime. With a Frontispiece and Cover Design by AUBREY BEARDSLEY. Small 4to. 7s. 6d. net.

FLEET STREET ECLOGUES. Fcap. 8vo, buckram. 4s. 6d. net.
[Third Edition.

FLEET STREET ECLOGUES. 2nd Series. Fcap. 8vo, buckram. 4s. 6d. net. *[Second Edition.*

A RANDOM ITINERARY AND A BALLAD. With a Frontispiece and Title-page by LAURENCE HOUSMAN. Fcap. 8vo, Irish Linen. 5s. net.

BALLADS AND SONGS. With a Title-page and Cover Design by WALTER WEST. Fcap. 8vo, buckram. 5s. net. *[Fourth Edition.*

NEW BALLADS. Fcap. 8vo, buckram. 4s. 6d. net. *[Second Edition.*

De Tabley (Lord).

POEMS, DRAMATIC AND LYRICAL. By JOHN LEICESTER WARREN (Lord de Tabley). Illustrations and Cover Design by C. S. RICKETTS. Crown 8vo. 7s. 6d. net. *[Third Edition.*

POEMS, DRAMATIC AND LYRICAL. Second Series, uniform in binding with the former volume. Crown 8vo. 5s. net.

Duer (Caroline, and Alice).

POEMS. Fcap. 8vo. 3s. 6d. net.

Egerton (George)

KEYNOTES. (*See* KEYNOTES SERIES.)

DISCORDS. (*See* KEYNOTES SERIES.)

YOUNG OFEG'S DITTIES. A translation from the Swedish of OLA HANSSON. With Title-page and Cover Design by AUBREY BEARDSLEY. Crown 8vo. 3s. 6d. net.

SYMPHONIES. *[In preparation.*

Eglinton (John).

TWO ESSAYS ON THE REMNANT. Post 8vo, wrappers. 1s. 6d net. *Transferred to the present Publisher.* [*Second Edition.*

Eve's Library.

Each volume, crown 8vo. 3s. 6d. net.

I. MODERN WOMEN. An English rendering of LAURA MARHOLM HANSSON'S "DAS BUCH DER FRAUEN" by HERMIONE RAMSDEN. Subjects: Sonia Kovalevsky, George Egerton, Eleanora Duse, Amalie Skram, Marie Bashkirtseff, A. Ch. Edgren Leffler.

II. THE ASCENT OF WOMAN. By ROY DEVEREUX.

III. MARRIAGE QUESTIONS IN MODERN FICTION. By ELIZABETH RACHEL CHAPMAN.

Fea (Allan).

THE FLIGHT OF THE KING: a full, true, and particular account of the escape of His Most Sacred Majesty King Charles II. after the Battle of Worcester, with Sixteen Portraits in Photogravure and nearly 100 other Illustrations. Demy 8vo. 21s. net.

Field (Eugene).

THE LOVE AFFAIRS OF A BIBLIOMANIAC. Post 8vo. 3s. 6d. net.

Fletcher (J. S.).

THE WONDERFUL WAPENTAKE. By "A SON OF THE SOIL." With 18 full-page Illustrations by J. A. SYMINGTON. Crown 8vo. 5s. 6d. net.

LIFE IN ARCADIA. (*See* ARCADY LIBRARY.)

GOD'S FAILURES. (*See* KEYNOTES SERIES.)

BALLADS OF REVOLT. Sq. 32mo. 2s. 6d. net.

Ford (James L.).

THE LITERARY SHOP AND OTHER TALES. Fcap. 8vo. 3s. 6d. net.

Four-and-Sixpenny Novels.

Each volume with Title-page and Cover Design by PATTEN WILSON. Crown 8vo. 4s. 6d. net.

GALLOPING DICK. By H. B. MARRIOTT WATSON.

THE WOOD OF THE BRAMBLES. By FRANK MATHEW.

THE SACRIFICE OF FOOLS. By R. MANIFOLD CRAIG.

A LAWYER'S WIFE. By Sir NEVILL GEARY, Bart. [*Second Edition.*

WEIGHED IN THE BALANCE. By HARRY LANDER.

GLAMOUR. By META ORRED.

PATIENCE SPARHAWK AND HER TIMES. By GERTRUDE ATHERTON.

THE WISE AND THE WAYWARD. By G. S. STREET.

The following are in preparation:

MIDDLE GREYNESS. By A. J. DAWSON.

DERELICTS. By W. J. LOCKE.

THE MARTYR'S BIBLE. By GEORGE FIFTH.

A CELIBATE'S WIFE. By HERBERT FLOWERDEW.

MAX. By JULIAN CROSKEY.

THE MAKING OF A PRIG. By EVELYN SHARP.

THE TREE OF LIFE. By NETTA SYRETT.

CECILIA. By STANLEY V. MAKOWER.

Fuller (H. B.).

THE PUPPET BOOTH. Twelve Plays. Crown 8vo. 4s. 6d. net.

Gale (Norman).

ORCHARD SONGS. With Title-page and Cover Design by J. ILLINGWORTH KAY. Fcap. 8vo, Irish Linen. 5s. net.

Also a Special Edition limited in number on hand-made paper bound in English vellum. £1 1s. net.

Garnett (Richard).

POEMS. With Title-page by J. ILLINGWORTH KAY. Crown 8vo. 5s. net.

DANTE, PETRARCH, CAMOENS, cxxiv Sonnets, rendered in English. With Title-page by PATTEN WILSON. Crown 8vo. 5s. net.

Gibson (Charles Dana).

DRAWINGS: Eighty-Five Large Cartoons. Oblong Folio. 15s. net.

Gibson (Charles Dana)—
continued.

PICTURES OF PEOPLE. Eighty-Five Large Cartoons. Oblong folio. 15s. net.

Gosse (Edmund).

THE LETTERS OF THOMAS LOVELL BEDDOES. Now first edited. Pott 8vo. 5s. net.

Also 25 copies large paper. 12s. 6d. net

Grahame (Kenneth).

PAGAN PAPERS. With Title-page by AUBREY BEARDSLEY. Fcap. 8vo. 5s. net.
[Out of Print at present.

THE GOLDEN AGE. With Cover Design by CHARLES ROBINSON. Crown 8vo. 3s. 6d. net.
[Fifth Edition.

Greene (G. A.).

ITALIAN LYRISTS OF TO-DAY. Translations in the original metres from about thirty-five living Italian poets, with bibliographical and biographical notes. Crown 8vo. 5s. net.

Greenwood (Frederick).

IMAGINATION IN DREAMS. Crown 8vo. 5s. net.

Hake (T. Gordon).

A SELECTION FROM HIS POEMS. Edited by Mrs. MEYNELL. With a Portrait after D. G. ROSSETTI, and a Cover Design by GLEESON WHITE. Crown 8vo. 5s. net.

Hayes (Alfred).

THE VALE OF ARDEN AND OTHER POEMS. With a Title-page and a Cover designed by E. H. NEW. Fcap. 8vo. 3s. 6d. net.

Also 25 copies large paper. 15s. net.

Hazlitt (William).

LIBER AMORIS; OR, THE NEW PYGMALION. Edited, with an Introduction, by RICHARD LE GALLIENNE. To which is added an exact transcript of the original MS., Mrs. Hazlitt's Diary in Scotland, and letters never before published. Portrait after BEWICK, and facsimile letters. 400 Copies only. 4to, 364 pp., buckram. 21s. net.

Heinemann (William).

THE FIRST STEP; A Dramatic Moment. Small 4to. 3s. 6d. net.

Hopper (Nora).

BALLAD IN PROSE. With a Title-page and Cover by WALTER WEST. Sq. 16mo. 5s. net.

UNDER QUICKEN BOUGHS. With Title-page designed by PATTEN WILSON, and Cover designed by ELIZABETH NAYLOR. Crown 8vo. 5s. net.

Housman (Clemence).

THE WERE WOLF. With 6 full-page Illustrations, Title-page, and Cover Design by LAURENCE HOUSMAN. Sq. 16mo. 3s. 6d. net.

Housman (Laurence).

GREEN ARRAS: Poems. With 6 Illustrations, Title-page, Cover Design, and End Papers by the Author. Crown 8vo. 5s. net.

GODS AND THEIR MAKERS. Crown 8vo, 3s. 6d. net. *[In preparation.*

Irving (Laurence).

GODEFROI AND YOLANDE: A Play. Sm. 4to. 3s. 6d. net.
[In preparation.

James (W. P.)

ROMANTIC PROFESSIONS: A Volume of Essays. With Title-page designed by J. ILLINGWORTH KAY. Crown 8vo. 5s. net.

Johnson (Lionel).

THE ART OF THOMAS HARDY: Six Essays. With Etched Portrait by WM. STRANG, and Bibliography by JOHN LANE. Crown 8vo. 5s. 6d. net. *[Second Edition.*

Also 150 copies, large paper, with proofs of the portrait. £1 1s. net.

Johnson (Pauline).

WHITE WAMPUM: Poems. With a Title-page and Cover Design by E. H. NEW. Crown 8vo. 5s. net.

Johnstone (C. E.).

BALLADS OF BOY AND BEAK. With a Title-page by F. H. TOWNSEND. Sq. 32mo. 2s. net.

Kemble (E. W.)

KEMBLE'S COONS. 30 Drawings of Coloured Children and Southern Scenes. Large 4to. 5s. net.

Keynotes Series.

Each volume with specially-designed Title-page by AUBREY BEARDSLEY or PATTEN WILSON. Crown 8vo, cloth. 3s. 6d. net.

I KEYNOTES. By GEORGE EGERTON.
[Seventh Edition.

II. THE DANCING FAUN. By FLORENCE FARR.

III. POOR FOLK. Translated from the Russian of F. Dostoievsky by LENA MILMAN. With a Preface by GEORGE MOORE.

IV. A CHILD OF THE AGE. By FRANCIS ADAMS.

V. THE GREAT GOD PAN AND THE INMOST LIGHT. By ARTHUR MACHEN.
[Second Edition.

VI. DISCORDS. By GEORGE EGERTON.
[Fifth Edition.

VII. PRINCE ZALESKI. By M. P. SHIEL.

VIII. THE WOMAN WHO DID. By GRANT ALLEN.
[Twenty-second Edition.

IX. WOMEN'S TRAGEDIES. By H. D. LOWRY.

X. GREY ROSES. By HENRY HARLAND.

XI. AT THE FIRST CORNER AND OTHER STORIES. By H. B. MARRIOTT WATSON.

XII. MONOCHROMES. By ELLA D'ARCY.

XIII. AT THE RELTON ARMS. By EVELYN SHARP.

XIV. THE GIRL FROM THE FARM. By GERTRUDE DIX.
[Second Edition.

XV. THE MIRROR OF MUSIC. By STANLEY V. MAKOWER.

XVI. YELLOW AND WHITE. By W. CARLTON DAWE.

XVII. THE MOUNTAIN LOVERS. By FIONA MACLEOD.

XVIII. THE WOMAN WHO DIDN'T. By VICTORIA CROSSE.
[Third Edition.

Keynotes Series—continued.

XIX. THE THREE IMPOSTORS. By ARTHUR MACHEN.

XX. NOBODY'S FAULT. By NETTA SYRETT.
[Second Edition.

XXI. THE BRITISH BARBARIANS. By GRANT ALLEN.
[Second Edition.

XXII. IN HOMESPUN. By E. NESBIT.

XXIII. PLATONIC AFFECTIONS. By JOHN SMITH.

XXIV. NETS FOR THE WIND. By UNA TAYLOR.

XXV. WHERE THE ATLANTIC MEETS THE LAND. By CALDWELL LIPSETT.

XXVI. IN SCARLET AND GREY. By FLORENCE HENNIKER. (With THE SPECTRE OF THE REAL by FLORENCE HENNIKER and THOMAS HARDY.) [Second Edition.

XXVII. MARIS STELLA. By MARIE CLOTHILDE BALFOUR.

XXVIII. DAY BOOKS. By MABEL E. WOTTON.

XXIX. SHAPES IN THE FIRE. By M. P. SHIEL.

XXX. UGLY IDOL. By CLAUD NICHOLSON.

XXXI. KAKEMONOS. By W. CARLTON DAWE.

XXXII. GOD'S FAILURES. By J. S. FLETCHER.

XXXIII. MERE SENTIMENT. By A. J. DAWSON.

XXXIV. A DELIVERANCE. By ALLAN MONKHOUSE.
[In preparation.

Lane's Library.

Each volume crown 8vo. 3s. 6d. net.

I. MARCH HARES. By HAROLD FREDERIC.
[Second Edition.

II. THE SENTIMENTAL SEX. By GERTRUDE WARDEN.

III. GOLD. By ANNIE LINDEN.

Lane's Library—*continued.*

The following are in preparation:

   IV. BROKEN AWAY. By BEATRICE GRIMSHAW.

   V. A MAN FROM THE NORTH. By E. A. BENNETT.

   VI. THE DUKE OF LINDEN. By JOSEPH F. CHARLES.

Leather (R. K.).

VERSES. 250 copies. Fcap. 8vo. 3s. net. [*Transferred to the present Publisher.*

Lefroy (Edward Cracroft.)

POEMS. With a Memoir by W. A. GILL, and a reprint of Mr. J. A. SYMONDS' Critical Essay on "Echoes from Theocritus." Cr. 8vo. Photogravure Portrait. 5s. net.

Le Gallienne (Richard).

PROSE FANCIES. With Portrait of the Author by WILSON STEER. Crown 8vo. Purple cloth. 5s. net. [*Fourth Edition.*

Also a limited large paper edition. 12s. 6d. net.

THE BOOK BILLS OF NARCISSUS. An Account rendered by RICHARD LE GALLIENNE. With a Frontispiece. Crown 8vo, purple cloth. 3s. 6d. net. [*Third Edition.*

Also 50 copies on large paper. 8vo. 10s. 6d. net.

ROBERT LOUIS STEVENSON, AN ELEGY, AND OTHER POEMS, MAINLY PERSONAL. With Etched Title-page by D. Y. CAMERON. Crown 8vo, purple cloth. 4s. 6d. net.

Also 75 copies on large paper. 8vo. 12s. 6d. net.

ENGLISH POEMS. Crown 8vo, purple cloth. 4s. 6d. net. [*Fourth Edition, revised.*

GEORGE MEREDITH: Some Characteristics. With a Bibliography (much enlarged) by JOHN LANE, portrait, &c. Crown 8vo, purple cloth. 5s. 6d. net. [*Fourth Edition.*

Le Gallienne (Richard)—*continued.*

THE RELIGION OF A LITERARY MAN. Crown 8vo, purple cloth. 3s. 6d. net. [*Fifth Thousand.* Also a special rubricated edition on hand-made paper. 8vo. 10s. 6d. net.

RETROSPECTIVE REVIEWS, A LITERARY LOG, 1891–1895. 2 vols. Crown 8vo, purple cloth. 9s. net.

PROSE FANCIES (Second Series). Crown 8vo, Purple cloth. 5s. net.

THE QUEST OF THE GOLDEN GIRL. Crown 8vo. 5s. net.

See also HAZLITT, WALTON and COTTON.

Lowry (H. D.).

MAKE BELIEVE. Illustrated by CHARLES ROBINSON. Crown 8vo, gilt edges or uncut. 5s. net.

WOMEN'S TRAGEDIES. (*See* KEYNOTES SERIES).

THE HAPPY EXILE. (*See* ARCADY LIBRARY).

Lucas (Winifred).

UNITS: Poems. Fcap. 8vo. 3s. 6d. net.

Lynch (Hannah).

THE GREAT GALEOTO AND FOLLY OR SAINTLINESS. Two Plays, from the Spanish of JOSÉ ECHEGARAY, with an Introduction. Small 4to. 5s. 6d. net.

Marzials (Theo.).

THE GALLERY OF PIGEONS AND OTHER POEMS. Post 8vo. 4s. 6d. net. [*Transferred to the present Publisher.*

The Mayfair Set.

Each volume fcap. 8vo. 3s. 6d. net.

   I. THE AUTOBIOGRAPHY OF A BOY. Passages selected by his friend G. S. STREET. With a Title-page designed by C. W. FURSE. [*Fifth Edition.*

   II. THE JONESES AND THE ASTERISKS. A Story in Monologue. By GERALD CAMPBELL. With a Title-page and 6 Illustrations by F. H. TOWNSEND. [*Second Edition.*

The Mayfair Set—*continued.*

III. SELECT CONVERSATIONS WITH AN UNCLE, NOW EXTINCT. By H. G. WELLS. With a Title-page by F. H. TOWNSEND.

IV. FOR PLAIN WOMEN ONLY. By GEORGE FLEMING. With a Title-page by PATTEN WILSON.

V. THE FEASTS OF AUTOLYCUS: THE DIARY OF A GREEDY WOMAN. Edited by ELIZABETH ROBINS PENNELL. With a Title-page by PATTEN WILSON.

VI. MRS. ALBERT GRUNDY: OBSERVATIONS IN PHILISTIA. By HAROLD FREDERIC. With a Title-page by PATTEN WILSON. [*Second Edition.*

Meredith (George).

THE FIRST PUBLISHED PORTRAIT OF THIS AUTHOR, engraved on the wood by W. BISCOMBE GARDNER, after the painting by G. F. WATTS. Proof copies on Japanese vellum, signed by painter and engraver. £1 1s. net.

Meynell (Mrs.).

POEMS. Fcap. 8vo. 3s. 6d. net. [*Fifth Edition.*

THE RHYTHM OF LIFE AND OTHER ESSAYS. Fcap. 8vo. 3s. 6d. net. [*Fifth Edition.*

THE COLOUR OF LIFE AND OTHER ESSAYS. Fcap 8vo. 3s. 6d. net. [*Fifth Edition.*

THE CHILDREN. Fcap. 8vo. 3s. 6d. net. [*Second Edition.*

Miller (Joaquin).

THE BUILDING OF THE CITY BEAUTIFUL. Fcap. 8vo. With a Decorated Cover. 5s. net.

Money-Coutts (F. B.).

POEMS. With Title-page designed by PATTEN WILSON. Crown 8vo. 3s. 6d. net.

Monkhouse (Allan).

BOOKS AND PLAYS: A Volume of Essays on Meredith, Borrow, Ibsen, and others. Crown 8vo. 5s. net.

A DELIVERANCE. (*See* KEYNOTES SERIES.)

Nesbit (E.).

A POMANDER OF VERSE. With a Title-page and Cover designed by LAURENCE HOUSMAN. Crown 8vo. 5s. net.

IN HOMESPUN. (*See* KEYNOTES SERIES.)

Nettleship (J. T.).

ROBERT BROWNING: Essays and Thoughts. Crown 8vo. 5s. 6d. net. [*Third Edition.*

Noble (Jas. Ashcroft).

THE SONNET IN ENGLAND AND OTHER ESSAYS. Title-page and Cover Design by AUSTIN YOUNG. Crown 8vo. 5s. net.

Also 50 copies large paper 12s. 6d. net

Oppenheim (Michael).

A HISTORY OF THE ADMINISTRATION OF THE ROYAL NAVY, and of Merchant Shipping in relation to the Navy from MDIX to MDCLX, with an introduction treating of the earlier period. With Illustrations. Demy 8vo. 15s. net.

O'Shaughnessy (Arthur).

HIS LIFE AND HIS WORK. With Selections from his Poems. By LOUISE CHANDLER MOULTON. Portrait and Cover Design. Fcap. 8vo. 5s. net.

Oxford Characters.

A series of lithographed portraits by WILL ROTHENSTEIN, with text by F. YORK POWELL and others. 200 copies only, folio, buckram. £3 3s. net.

25 special large paper copies containing proof impressions of the portraits signed by the artist, £6 6s. net.

Peters (Wm. Theodore).

POSIES OUT OF RINGS. With Title-page by PATTEN WILSON. Sq. 16mo. 2s. 6d. net.

Pierrot's Library.

Each volume with Title-page, Cover and End Papers, designed by AUBREY BEARDSLEY. Sq. 16mo. 2s. net.

I. PIERROT. By H. DE VERE STACPOOLE.
II. MY LITTLE LADY ANNE. By Mrs. EGERTON CASTLE.
III. SIMPLICITY. By A. T. G. PRICE.
IV. MY BROTHER. By VINCENT BROWN.

The following are in preparation:

V. DEATH, THE KNIGHT, AND THE LADY. By H. DE VERE STACPOOLE.
VI. MR. PASSINGHAM. By THOMAS COBB.
VII. TWO IN CAPTIVITY. By VINCENT BROWN.

Plarr (Victor).

IN THE DORIAN MOOD: Poems. With Title-page by PATTEN WILSON. Crown 8vo. 5s. net.

Posters in Miniature: over

250 reproductions of French, English and American Posters with Introduction by EDWARD PENFIELD. Large crown 8vo. 5s. net.

Radford (Dollie).

SONGS AND OTHER VERSES. With a Title-page by PATTEN WILSON. Fcap. 8vo. 4s. 6d. net.

Rhys (Ernest).

A LONDON ROSE AND OTHER RHYMES. With Title-page designed by SELWYN IMAGE. Crown 8vo. 5s. net.

Robertson (John M.).

ESSAYS TOWARDS A CRITICAL METHOD. (New Series.) Crown 8vo. 5s. net. [*In preparation.*

St. Cyres (Lord).

THE LITTLE FLOWERS OF ST. FRANCIS: A new rendering into English of the Fioretti di San Francesco. Crown 8vo. 5s. net. [*In preparation.*

Seaman (Owen).

THE BATTLE OF THE BAYS. Fcap. 8vo. 3s. 6d. net.

Sedgwick (Jane Minot).

SONGS FROM THE GREEK. Fcap. 8vo. 3s. 6d. net.

Setoun (Gabriel).

THE CHILD WORLD: Poems. With over 200 Illustrations by CHARLES ROBINSON. Crown 8vo, gilt edges or uncut. 5s. net.

Sharp (Evelyn).

WYMPS: Fairy Tales. With Coloured Illustrations by MABEL DEARMER. Small 4to, decorated cover. 4s. 6d. net.

AT THE RELTON ARMS. (*See* KEYNOTES SERIES.)

THE MAKING OF A PRIG. (*See* FOUR-AND-SIXPENNY NOVELS.)

Shore (Louisa).

POEMS. With an appreciation by FREDERIC HARRISON and a Portrait. Fcap. 8vo. 5s. net.

Short Stories Series.

Each volume Post 8vo. Coloured edges. 2s. 6d. net.

I. SOME WHIMS OF FATE. By MÉNIE MURIEL DOWIE.
II. THE SENTIMENTAL VIKINGS. By R. V. RISLEY.
III. SHADOWS OF LIFE. By Mrs. MURRAY HICKSON.

Stevenson (Robert Louis).

PRINCE OTTO. A Rendering in French by EGERTON CASTLE. With Frontispiece, Title-page, and Cover Design by D. Y. CAMERON. Crown 8vo. 7s. 6d. net.

Also 50 copies on large paper, uniform in size with the Edinburgh Edition of the Works.

A CHILD'S GARDEN OF VERSES. With over 150 Illustrations by CHARLES ROBINSON. Crown 8vo. 5s. net. [*Second Edition.*

Stimson (F. J.)

KING NOANETT. A Romance of Devonshire Settlers in New England. Illustrated. Large crown 8vo. 5s. net.

Stoddart (Thos. Tod).

THE DEATH WAKE. With an Introduction by ANDREW LANG. Fcap. 8vo. 5s. net.

Street (G. S.).
EPISODES. Post 8vo. 3s. net.
MINIATURES AND MOODS. Fcap.
8vo. 3s. net. [Both transferred
to the present Publisher.
QUALES EGO: A FEW REMARKS,
IN PARTICULAR AND AT LARGE.
Fcap. 8vo. 3s. 6d. net.
THE AUTOBIOGRAPHY OF A BOY.
(See MAYFAIR SET.)
THE WISE AND THE WAYWARD.
(See FOUR - AND - SIXPENNY
NOVELS.)

Swettenham (F. A.)
MALAY SKETCHES. With a Title-
page and Cover Design by PATTEN
WILSON. Crown 8vo. 5s. net.
[Second Edition.

Tabb (John B.).
POEMS. Sq. 32mo. 4s. 6d. net.

Tennyson (Frederick).
POEMS OF THE DAY AND YEAR.
With a Title-page designed by
PATTEN WILSON. Crown 8vo.
5s. net.

Thimm (Carl A.).
A COMPLETE BIBLIOGRAPHY OF
FENCING AND DUELLING, AS
PRACTISED BY ALL EUROPEAN
NATIONS FROM THE MIDDLE
AGES TO THE PRESENT DAY.
With a Classified Index, arranged
Chronologically according to
Languages. Illustrated with
numerous Portraits of Ancient
and Modern Masters of the Art.
Title-pages and Frontispieces of
some of the earliest works. Por-
trait of the Author by WILSON
STEER, and Title page designed
by PATTEN WILSON. 4to. 21s.
net.

Thompson (Francis)
POEMS. With Frontispiece, Title-
page, and Cover Design by
LAURENCE HOUSMAN. Pott 4to.
5s. net. [Fourth Edition.
SISTER-SONGS: An Offering to
Two Sisters. With Frontispiece,
Title-page, and Cover Design by
LAURENCE HOUSMAN. Pott 4to.
5s. net.

Thoreau (Henry David).
POEMS OF NATURE. Selected and
edited by HENRY S. SALT and
FRANK B. SANBORN, with a
Title-page designed by PATTEN
WILSON. Fcap. 8vo. 4s. 6d.
net.

Traill (H. D.).
THE BARBAROUS BRITISHERS: A
Tip-top Novel. With Title and
Cover Design by AUBREY
BEARDSLEY. Crown 8vo, wrap-
per. 1s. net.
FROM CAIRO TO THE SOUDAN
FRONTIER. With Cover Design
by PATTEN WILSON. Crown
8vo. 5s. net.

Tynan Hinkson (Katharine)
CUCKOO SONGS. With Title-page
and Cover Design by LAURENCE
HOUSMAN. Fcap. 8vo. 5s. net.
MIRACLE PLAYS. OUR LORD'S
COMING AND CHILDHOOD. With
6 Illustrations, Title-page, and
Cover Design by PATTEN WIL-
SON. Fcap. 8vo. 4s. 6d. net.

Walton and Cotton.
THE COMPLEAT ANGLER. Edited
by RICHARD LE GALLIENNE.
Illustrated by EDMUND H. NEW.
Fcap. 4to, decorated cover. 15s.
net.
Also to be had in thirteen 1s parts.

Watson (Rosamund Mar-
riott).
VESPERTILIA AND OTHER POEMS.
With a Title-page designed by R.
ANNING BELL. Fcap 8vo. 4s. 6d.
net.
A SUMMER NIGHT AND OTHER
POEMS. New Edition. With a
Decorative Title-page. Fcap.
8vo. 3s. net.

Watson (William).
THE FATHER OF THE FOREST AND
OTHER POEMS. With New Photo-
gravure Portrait of the Author
Fcap. 8vo, buckram. 3s. 6d. net.
[Fifth Edition.
ODES AND OTHER POEMS. Fcap.
8vo, buckram. 4s. 6d. net.
[Fourth Edition.

Watson (William)—*continued.*

THE ELOPING ANGELS: A Caprice Square 16mo, buckram. 3s. 6d. net. [*Second Edition.*

EXCURSIONS IN CRITICISM : being some Prose Recreations of a Rhymer. Crown 8vo, buckram. 5s. ret. [*Second Edition.*

THE PRINCE'S QUEST AND OTHER POEMS. With a Bibliographical Note added. Fcap. 8vo, buckram. 4s. 6d. net. [*Third Edition.*

THE PURPLE EAST: A Series of Sonnets on England's Desertion of Armenia. With a Frontispiece after G. F. WATTS, R.A. Fcap. 8vo, wrappers. 1s. net. [*Third Edition.*

THE YEAR OF SHAME. With an Introduction by the BISHOP OF HEREFORD. Fcap. 8vo. 2s. 6d. net. [*Second Edition.*

Watt (Francis).

THE LAW'S LUMBER ROOM. Fcap. 8vo. 3s. 6d. net. [*Second Edition.*

Watts-Dunton (Theodore).

POEMS. Crown 8vo. 5s. net. [*In preparation.*

There will also be an *Edition de Luxe* of this volume printed at the Kelmscott Press.

Wenzell (A. B.)

IN VANITY FAIR. 70 Drawings. Oblong folio. 15s. net.

Wharton (H. T.)

SAPPHO. Memoir, Text, Selected Renderings, and a Literal Translation by HENRY THORNTON WHARTON. With 3 Illustrations in Photogravure, and a Cover designed by AUBREY BEARDSLEY. Fcap. 8vo. 7s. 6d. net. [*Third Edition.*

THE YELLOW BOOK

An Illustrated Quarterly.

Pott 4to.   5s. net.

I. April 1894, 272 pp., 15 Illustrations. [*Out of print.*

II. July 1894, 364 pp., 23 Illustrations.

III. October 1894, 280 pp., 15 Illustrations.

IV. January 1895, 285 pp., 16 Illustrations.

V. April 1895, 317 pp., 14 Illustrations.

VI. July 1895, 335 pp., 16 Illustrations.

VII. October 1895, 320 pp., 20 Illustrations.

VIII. January 1896, 406 pp., 26 Illustrations.

IX. April 1896, 256 pp., 17 Illustrations.

X. July 1896, 340 pp., 13 Illustrations.

XI. October 1896, 342 pp., 12 Illustrations.

XII. January 1897, 350 pp., 14 Illustrations.